BIHAR

DARBHANGA
• MUZAFFARPUR
• CHANDI
PATNA • MONGHYR
BIHAR • BHAGALPUR
NAWADA
• GAYA
DHANBAD
RANCHI •
JAMSHEDPUR

GUJARAT

• BHUJ MEHSANA
⊙AHMADABAD
• NADIAD
• JAMNAGAR
• RAJKOT • VADODARA
PORBANDAR
BHAVNAGAR
SURAT
• BARDOLI

PROTEST MOVEMENTS
IN TWO INDIAN STATES

PUBLICATIONS OF
THE CENTRE FOR SOCIAL STUDIES,
SURAT

1. *Primary Education in Surat District*, (1970) by Y.D. Jadeja
2. *Glimpses of Surat*, (1972) by I.P. Desai
3. *Water Facilities for Untouchables in Gujarat*, (1973) by I P. Desai
4. *Untouchability in Rural Gujarat*, (1976) by I. P. Desai
5. *History of Rural Development in Modern India*, (1977) by I. P. Desai and Banwarilal Chaudhari
6. *Politics of Scheduled Castes and Tribes*,(1975) by Ghanshyam Shah
7. *Caste Association and Political Process in Gujarat*, (1975) by Ghanshyam Shah
8. *Protest Movements in Two Indian States*, (1977)) by Ghanshyam Shah
9. *Bureaucracy and Development*, (1975) by Ramashray Roy.

PROTEST MOVEMENTS
IN TWO INDIAN STATES

A STUDY OF THE GUJARAT AND
BIHAR MOVEMENTS

GHANSHYAM SHAH

AJANTA PUBLICATIONS (INDIA)

1st Published June, 1977

by

S. BALWANT

for

AJANTA PUBLICATIONS (India), DELHI-7

Distributors :

AJANTA BOOKS INTERNATIONAL
1-U.B., Jawahar Nagar, Bungalow Road,
Post Box, 2194, Delhi-110007

Printed by Prakash Type Setters at Radiant Printers,
West Patel Nagar, New Delhi-12.

In Memory of
NARENDRABHAI MEHTA

PREFACE

The year 1974 was a year of unprecedented turmoil in the history of post-Independence India. The deepening economic crises combined with weakening legitimacy of political institutions produced a situation in which disturbances, and even sporadic rioting, in several parts of the country became not uncommon. This had its clumination in Gujarat and in Bihar. The Gujarat agitation of January-March 1974 ended in the dissolution of the state Assembly. It achieved its specific goal. In Bihar, the agitation began in March 1974 with the slogan "Bihar bhi Gujarat Banega" (Gujarat will be repeated in Bihar). It spilled over to 1975. Unlike the Gujarat agitation, Bihar agitation had an organization, with a central guiding authority of Bihar Chhatra Sangharsh Samiti, planned programmes, a cadre and the leadership of Jayaprakash Narayan.

The Gujarat agitation and the Bihar movement have far reaching consequences for Indian politics. They have raised certain basic questions regarding the political system and the type of future Indian society. That provided us a focus of inquiry. We have concerned with the "total revolution" aspect of the Bihar movement. The scope of both the studies is limited to examine the nature of two agitations. Analysis of the issues raised in the course of agitations, identification of the actors and the participants, and their role etc. are all directed at understanding the concept of "total revolution".

The report entitled the "Upsurge in Gujarat" was written in April 1974, soon after the dissolution of the Assembly, and was published in *Economic and Political Weekly* in August 1974. It is being presented here as it appeared in the journal except for some editorial changes. The political events in Gujarat between March 1974 and June 1975 confirm the analysis of that report and it was not necessary to rewrite it.

The study of the Bihar movement covers the first year—from March 1974 to 1975—of the movement. The report was completed on the eve of the Emergency. Since then many political changes have taken place in the country. The Congress has lost power at the Centre and the new Union government enjoys the support of the Sarvodaya and other activists of the Bihar movement. The analysis presented in the Bihar report is still valid today, and I do not feel any need to change it. Hence, the report presented here is the same as it was written before the Emergency, except for the necessary change in the tense. I have added a prostscript to make the account up-dated.

The Bihar study could not see the light of the day during the Emergency. Publishers were not ready to take the risk. Recently, the *Economic and Political Weekly* serialise the report in some what abridged form in April, 1977. I thank the *Economic and Political Weekly* for its permission to republish the Gujarat and Bihar studies.

I.P. Desai with whom I have been associated for the last five years, has helped me in understanding the realities of our society. Thanks to my association with him, I have unlearned many things which would have thwarted my development. He read drafts of both the studies and offered valuable comments. I have no words to express my gratitude to him.

I am also thankful to Rajni Kothari, Jeffrey Ostergaard, S.P. Punalekar, W.H. Moris Jones, D.L. Sheth, J.K. Desai and David Hardiman who read the earlier drafts of both or either of the reports and gave candid suggestions.

My thanks are due to A.N. Sinha Intsitute of Social Studies, Patna for providing me accommodation and other facilities during my stay in Patna, and to Ali Ashraf and Gopikrishna Prasad for their various acts of kindness. I must thank, several Sarvodaya workers and other activists of Bihar movement who replied to my querries frankly and thus enabled me to understand many aspects of the movement. I apologize to them if their feeling are hurt by the analysis presented here. I also thank K.M. Bhavsar for typing the reports and M.C. Dordi for preparing the map.

I owe special thanks to the Indian Council of Social Science Research, New Delhi, for its very prompt decision to sanction a grant to carry out the Bihar study. Although I received help from many friends, the analysis of the movements presented in the book are mine and no one else is responsible for the views expressed.

Moving about the tension-torn areas in the course of these studies involved some physical risks. My wife and children were in constant anxiety during my field trips in Gujarat and Bihar. Thereafter, while writing the reports I often neglected their legitimate demands on my time. But they forbid me to publicly acknowledge my debt to them.

—Ghanshyam Shah

CONTENTS

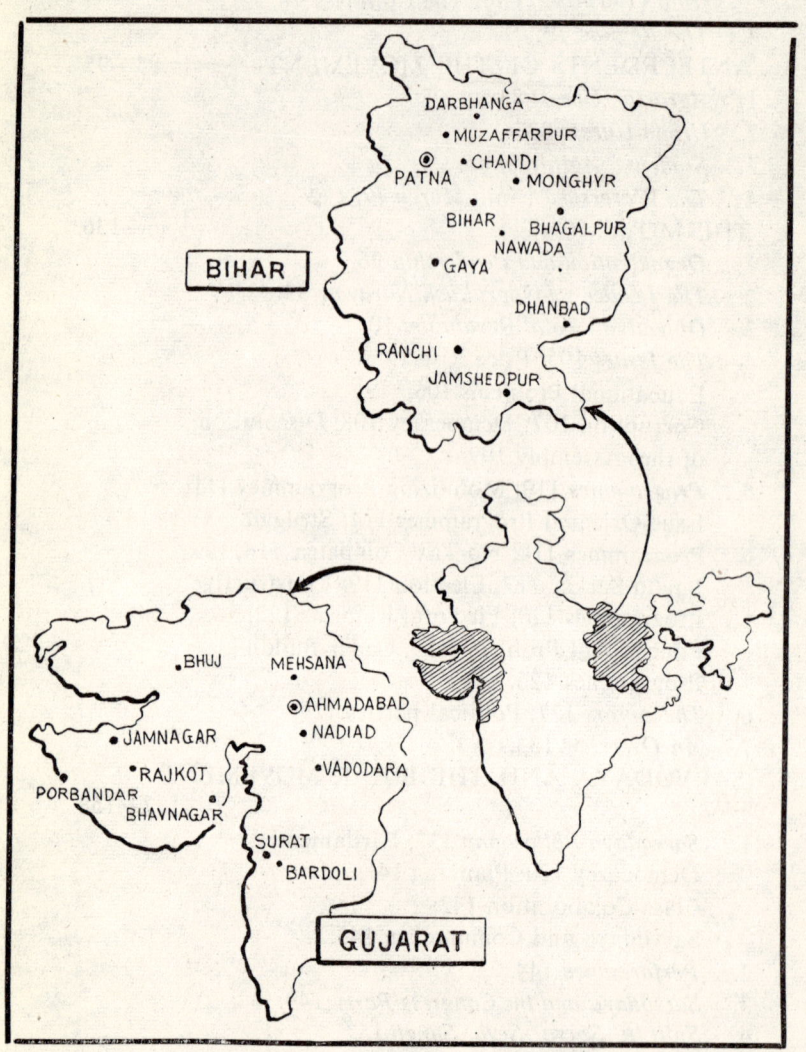

GUJARAT

Introduction

The political upheaval which shook Gujarat for full two months in 1974 was unprecedented in the history of post-independence India. No town remained untouched by the upsurge. Tensions also prevailed in some parts of the country-side.

Spearheaded by the student community, the agitation took various forms such as processions, demonstrations, fasts, gheraos, bandhs, stone-throwing, hijacking of buses, and looting and burning of private and public property—including colleges, court and municipal buildings, milk booths, provision shops, grain godowns, cloth shops, tea stalls, and pan shops. Prohibitory orders, arrests, tear-gassing, lathi charges and even firings failed to stem the tide of people's wrath against the government. During the agitation about one hundred persons were killed and a large number injured in police firings at different places. Some policemen and officers were also wounded in incidents of stone-throwing; stray attempts were made to snatch away rifles from the police personnel.

The Chief Minister, Chimanbhai Patel, despite his claim of having a majority in the State Assembly, resigned on February 9, 1974. The Assembly was suspended, and President's rule was imposed on the state. Later, 95 of the 168 MLAs resigned from the House. Consequently, the Central government was compelled to dissolve the Assembly on March 15, 1974. Corporators of Ahmedabad, Baroda, and Surat resigned *en bloc*, and the municipal Corporations were superseded. Several Congressmen resigned from the party.

Different socio-economic and political groups participated in the agitation for different purposes, raising issues like corruption, blackmarketing, price rise, denationalization, rationing, civil liberties, injustice to Gujaratis and Gujarat, etc. But finally all the purposes converged on two common demands, resignation of the Chief Minister and, later, dissolution of the State Assembly. The reasons for making these demands differed from group to group. For the majority of the agitators, it was to overthrow 'corrupt' politicians. The opposition political parties were interested in dethroning the Congress party in the state, which they had not succeeded in doing by constitutional means. Some were interested in discrediting the 'progressive measures', such as the wheat trade take-over, land legislations, etc., of the ruling party. Some groups considered the demands as marking the transition to socio-economic change. Some wanted to establish partyless democracy. Consequently there was neither unity nor clarity regarding the steps to be taken after the dissolution of the Assembly.

The upsurge has been viewed differently by different persons and groups. To some, it was a 'fascist' movement or a 'counter-revolution'. To others it was a revolution or at least the pre-revolutionary stage. Some branded it as a 'Naxalite' movement. Some saw in the agitation the shape of things to come— chaos and turmoil in the country as a whole. It is not our intention to examine these views and the theories, or lack of theories, behind these views. The present monograph is an attempt to note the major events or incidents with a view to understanding the agitation as a social phenomenon. The monograph seeks to examine the following questions : What role did the different groups play in accelerating the agitation ? How and why did the agitation take different shapes at different stages ? Which issues were highlighted by which groups and why ?

The monograph is an exploratory study based on interviews with those who participated in the agitation, on survey data, newspaper reports as well as the writer's own observations. The monograph is divided into two parts : In the first part, I have dealt in detail with the prevailing tensions in Gujarat state. In the second part, the nature of the agitation and the character of the participants have been described.

Discontent, Tensions and Politics

In order to understand the agitation, one needs to examine the socio-economic and political under-currents in the state. What follows is a broad outline of the prevailing tensions in general, and in urban areas in particular. We shall then proceed to examine the nature of the different sections of society and the political situation in the state.

1. DISCONTENT AND TENSIONS

According to the 1971 census, 28 per cent of the population of Gujarat, as against the all-India average of 20 per cent, live in urban areas. The concentration is in the larger-sized towns : according to the 1961 census, 52.97 per cent of the urban population lived in Class I (100,000 and over population) and Class II (50,000 to 99,999 population) towns. These were in all 7 Class I and 18 Class II towns. This proportion had gone up to 60.76 per cent according the 1971 census. In the Class I and II towns the density of population is 8,216.20 and 4,402.24 per sq km respectively. The overcrowded towns do not have adequate civic amenities like water, drainage, health services, transport etc.[1]

The Centre for Regional Development Studies, Surat, conducted a survey just before the agitation, between December 25, 1973 and Jaunary 10, 1974, in Surat to get an idea of prevailing tensions in urban areas. Surat is the second largest city in Gujarat. In this section, we shall make use of the data of Surat survey to explain the prevailing tensions.[2]

In order to understand the problems of the city and the people's cognition of the civic problems, a question was asked :

"According to you, what are the major problems of the city ?"
Leaving out the one out of four persons who could not think
of a problem either because he was too comfortable or because
he lacked the cognitive capacity to articulate the problems of
the city, a large number of persons (more then 50 per cent)
interviewed indicated price rise and scarcity as the major
problem of the city. This highlights the economic hardships
of the people.

Next to price rise, people considered transport to be a
major problem of the city. Besides irregular and overcrowded
buses, people often had to wait for more than an hour to catch
a bus. Consequently, frenquent confrontations between members
of the middle class (particularly students and youth) and bus
conductors took place during the last two years in several cities
of Gujarat. It may be noted that only 48 per cent of the total
transport buses of Ahmedabad run regularly on roads.[3]

The prices of essential commodities had sharply increased
during 1973. Though the prices came down slightly after the
July riots in Ahmedabad, they shot up again after August 1973
despite a bumper crop. The prices of foodgrains, edible oil,
ghee, vegetables and meat rose from 30 to more than 100 per
cent during the previous year.

Besides, milk cost Rs. 2 per litre. A cup of tea in restaurants cost 35 to 40 paise. A loaf of bread weighing 450 grams
cost one rupee. Charges for a limited "thali" for lunch were
Rs. 2. One had to pay not less than Rs. 110 per month for
two meals a day. Ordinarily snacks, even in cheap eating
places, cost at least one rupee. One could not afford to eat
chana (gram) and *sing* (groundnut) which cost 80 paise for a
hundred grammes.

Certain commodities not only became costly but also disappeared from the market. For instance, oil, ghee, butter,
baby-foods, kerosene, etc, were not to be found in the open
market. Foodgrains like wheat and rice also became scarce.

Gujarat is deficit in foodgrains. It depends on the
Centre for feeding the people. The state found itself in a
precarious situation following a drastic cut in the supply
of foodgrains by the Centre after June 1973. As against its
monthly requirement of 1,00,000 tonnes of wheat, the state
got only 15,000 tonnes a month in November and December.[4]

When we break down these figures at district level the gravity of the food situation becomes clearer. Take, for example, Surat city and district. There were 16,29,000 and 4,43,000 ration card-holders in the district and city, respectively. The total supply of foodgrains including wheat, jowar, milo and rice was 10,000 tonnes in May. As months passed, the quota was reduced drastically, reaching 2,770 tonnes in the month of December (Table 1). Similarly, in the case of wheat it was 6,900 tonnes in May ; in August, it was reduced to 1,800 tonnes, and in November it was reduced to 1,200 to 1,100 tonnes. The same was the position as regards jowar. In the case of rice it was even worse. In May, the supply was 1,000 tonnes which declined to 70 tonnes in December.

TABLE 1. : Food Supply In Surat District in 1973

(in tonnes)

Food-grains	May	June	July	August	Sept.	Oct.	Nov.	Dec.
Wheat	6900	6600	4500	1800	1500	2000	1200	1100
Jowar	100	...	...	...	1500	...	...	...
Milo	1500	700	2500	1200	...	3000	1800	1600
Rice	1000	894	450	...	...	100	155	70
Total	10000	8194	7450	3000	3000	5100	3155	2770

Source : Gujarat Mitra, December 30, 1973.

Consequently, a card-holder got only one kilogram of wheat per month per head in November and December from the ration shops. Rice was not distributed at all. A card-holder got two kilograms of jowar. The quality of food-grains in the ration shop was also bad. The grains were full of dust and stones and one had to spend at least two to three hours to clean the grain. The poor quality and the meagre quantity of foodgrains forced poor persons to buy from the open market where prices of the commodities were twice as high.

The steep price rise and scarcity of essential commodities had, thus, broken the common man's back. In Surat, for instance, about 66 per cent of the families earned less than Rs. 300 per month. On a fairly conservative reckoning, the expenses of a family of four persons came to Rs. 150 on foodgrains and other household items like soap, edible oil, sugar, etc, Rs. 30 for milk (half a litre per day), Rs. 10 for transport, Rs. 30 for vegetables, Rs. 30 for rent including electricity and water, and the remaining Rs. 50 for tea and canteen, clothes, medicine, observing social customs, and a minimum of entertainment like a visit to a cinema. One could imagine the strain on such families. And these were in fact the relatively better off families. The condition of persons like clerks, typists, Class IV employees, accountants and salesmen in private firms and shops and casual labourers, earning Rs. 200 or less per month, was miserable. Their condition was more pathetic since they lived alone in the cities, without their families (as about 10 per cent of the working population in the cities do). Because of the steep rise in the prices of all commodities, they could not save anything and so cannot send anything to their dependants back home. Without family bonds and discipline on the one hand, and faced with economic hardships on the other, such people are susceptible to being drawn into any mob action.

CONSUMERS AND TRADERS

There is a continuous conflict between consumers and traders in urban areas, with the former becoming more vocal and conscious of their rights. The conflict had become sharper in 1974 as a result of rising prices and scarcity of commodities on the one hand, and incipient consumer movement on the other. There was a general impression among the people that shopkeepers were blackmarketeers and profiteers. Take the example of Surat city. It was found in our survey that every third person had a feeling that he was continuously being cheated by shopkeepers; another 40 per cent felt that they were being cheated sometimes. Thus three-fourths of the population did not trust traders. Further, 76 per cent of the respondents reported that they constantly felt that they got adulterated material from the market. They alleged that in order to make more profit the shopkeepers mixed all sorts of adulterants with commodities and thus played with the lives of the people.

The profiteering attitude and arrogance of the shopkeepers

was obvious during the riots too. In between the two curfew periods people rushed to do their shopping. Shopkeepers took advantage of this situation and charged higher prices. Sometimes this brought the conflict between the customers and the shopkeepers into the open and some customers looted some shops in retaliation.

FRUSTRATION AND POWERLESSNESS

"The economic situation is worsening and we do not know what will happen tomorrow......We voted for Indira Gandhi in the hope that she would do something for the common man, but she has not done anything. Prices are rising everyday and it is difficult to live on our meagre means." This is what a white-collar worker, earning Rs. 250 per month, had to say. His feelings were widely shared. An overwhelming number of persons (91 per cent) felt that the living condition of the common man had not improved in the last two decades. On the contrary many of them (70 per cent) felt that it had actually deteriorated. The picture of the future presented by these respondents was also very gloomy. As many as 84 per cent of the urban dwellers felt that their children would have to face greater hardships than they.

In addition to economic strains and frustration, a large number of people found themselves powerless in their relationship with the political system. This is evident from Table 2.

TABLE 2 : Alienation and Powerlessness

Items	Percentages
1. Cannot meet officials directly	74
2. Cannot do anything to make the city better	65
3. Find government and politics so complex that one cannot understand what is going on	88
4. Representatives do not pay attention to the problems of the people	88
5. Officials do not pay attention to what persons like me say	91

Seven out of ten persons expressed their inability to meet officials directly. They also felt that they could not do anything for the development of the city. The number of persons feeling helpless increased when asked about the effectiveness with government officials and elected representatives. Nine out of ten persons felt that neither elected representatives nor officials paid any attention to the problems of the common man. They were not being listened to by the government officials or politicians. They found themselves powerless in their personal lives as well as in the socio-political system.

People's frustration and helplessness need to be examined in the context of the present political system. This needs a separate and more elaborate study than is possible in the present inquiry. However, from our data we are able to present a few aspects which may indicate the trend. It is found that 40 per cent of our urban respondents had lost faith in elections. They felt that elections were deceptive. Only men of influence and money could fight the elections. After the elections, according to them, the leaders did not care for the electorate. Politicians only looked after their own interests and the interests of their respective groups.

With faith in the electoral system shaken, many persons advocated the need for direct action. Of the respondents of Surat, 67 per cent considered strikes, gheraos, dharnas, etc. legitimate and necessary to secure their demands. And 22 per cent of the respondents accepted violence as either inevitable or as the last resort to solve their problems. This is not an insignificant number. After all, only a few persons actually participate in violent activities (as seen in the recent riots).

The above evidence suggests that an overwhelming proportion of the people were frustrated, found themselves helples , and were losing faith in the present political system. They opted for direct action to solve their problems.

2. DIFFERENT SOCIAL GROUPS AND THEIR PROBLEMS

Though unrest prevailed among all sections of society, the causes of discontent differed from group to group. In order to understand the nature and process of the turmoil that took place in Gujarat, it is necessary to delineate the nature of the various groups and their problems.

INDUSTRIALISTS AND BIG BUSINESSMEN

Industrialists or big businessmen are not affected by the steep price rise or corrupt politics. They are highly organized and are in a position to assert their interests through organizations like the Millowners' Association, the Chamber of Commerce, Manufacturers', Associations, Wholesale Grain Merchants' Association, the Mahajans (Guilds), etc. And local associations are linked with state and national level organizations. As a group they support the party and the action which is in power. They give financial support to the Swatantra party as well as the ruling Congress. They oblige ministers, members of the legislature, and have no difficulty in "getting things done". What they cannot influence at the policy level, they manage to secure at the implementation level. Their hold on the ruling party and on the administration is beyond doubt.

Groundnut oil dealers are well organized in Gujarat. In order to extract a higher profit, they are interested in exporting oil to other states. They smuggle out oil on a large scale to escape excise duty. The government has always succumbed to the oil dealers in one way or another. It was reported in the Press that the oil dealers gave large amounts to individual politicians of the ruling party and to party funds for elections. These dealers were strong supporters of Chimanbhai Patel. At a meeting between oil dealers and the government in October 1973, the Chief Minister is reported to have said : "You know my interests and I know your interests. You protect my interests and I will protect your interests." Soon after this meeting, the prices of groundnut oil, which had shown a declining trend, shot up sharply. Moreover, in November the government gave up the practice of procuring oil through levy from groundnut oil mills. This also worked to the advantage of oil dealers. Nor was the government strict towards hoarders and black-marketeers.

Individually, businessmen and industrialists are in competition with each other in business and public life. For status as well as patronage some of them sponsor educational institutions and several other voluntary associations. A few of them have also sponsored or support different political parties—Swantantra, Congress (O), Congress (R) and the Jana Sangh.

According to them, all the four political parties, though they differ in their postures, support different groups within the parties. And different industrialists spare no effort to bring men belonging to the groups they support to power and to keep them there in the face of opposition from their competitors. However, all of them are bitterly opposed to the 'radicals' the pro-poor politicians who are openly against business interest. For instance, during the recent events in Gujarat, the industrialists and the other rich persons were divided as supporters or opponents of Chiman Patel, Amul Desai, Ghiya, Adani, Oza or Thakorbhai Patel according to what at any moment suited their diverse personal interests. But they were all against Jhinabhai Darji, the President of the Gujarat Congress, who had refused to succumb to the demands of rich businessmen and industrialists who play a significant role in faction fights within the ruling party.

RICH PEASANTS

A section of the peasants has become prosperous during the last two decades. Thanks to irrigation facilities, fertilizers, new seeds and transport facilities and thanks to the enormous demand for cash crops in which the prosperous peasantry of central and south Gujarat specializes, the peasants have become very rich and very powerful politically. And they are no longer mere peasants; through their control of government and the co-operative credit institutions, they have become big entrepreneurs as well. They have thus been linked with urban businessmen and industrialists.

During the independence movement, the peasants of central and south Gujarat launched agitations against the British government to oppose land revenue. And since independence, they have been organized under different names. Bhailalbhai Patel, a leading Patidar leader of Kheda district and the founder of Vallabh Vidyanagar, organized a political party, Khedut Sangh, in 1952 to oppose land legislation. In 1968, the peasant interest in the Swatantra and Congress parties organized the Khedut Mandal outside their parties. And in 1973, the Khedut Samaj, under the leadership of Dayaram Patel of south Gujarat, Vallabhbhai Patel of Saurashtra, and Ambubhai Patel of north

Gujarat, came into existence to oppose 'progressive' land legislation. Besides, cotton growers and others have set up their
respective organizations and have worked as powerful lobbies
within the Congress in Ahmedabad and New Delhi. Like the
industrialists and rich businessmen, the rich peasants maintain
good relations with the faction in power. Their hold on the
administration too is strong. Land legislation has so far not
been able to make much impact at the implementation level.
And whatever surplus land has been acquired under the Acts
has gone largely to the upper and middle castes. The condition of small farmers and landless labourers has remained more
or less the same as before.

The Khedut Samaj had become active in the latter part of
1973 against the proposed land ceiling bill as well as the levy
on paddy. In October, the Samaj organized meetings, processions and demonstrations against the land ceiling bill. It
organized a huge rally at Gandhinagar where a confrontation
took place between police and demonstrators. A procession
of teenaged sons and daughters of the farmers was organized
in New Delhi which submitted a memorandum to the Prime
Minister, demanding protection of the minors' rights in land.
The Kheduts also organized morchas and gheraos against
MLAs and tried to persuade them to resign from the State
Assembly. In some villages, peasants boycotted government
works. These peasants threw their weight behind Sardar
Patel's daughter, Maniben Patel, the Congress (O) candidate,
in the election.

The government did not scrap the land ceiling bill, but at
the same time it did not want to go against the peasants. It
is interesting to note here that barring four or five members,
all the Congress legislators favoured raising of the ceiling. The
government rejected a suggestion of a Congress MLA that
agricultural land be taken over from so-called farmers whose
non-agricultural annual income was more than Rs. 15,000.
The government also rejected even the simple suggestion of
forming a watchdog committee to oversee the implementation
of the bill.[5] Nor did the government take any other steps to
gear up the administrative machinery to implement the
bill. And the peasants took a pledge in public that surplus
land would not be surrendered to the government for distribu-

tion among the landless under the land ceiling Act. A leader of the Samaj audaciously said at a public meeting that the Act was not going to be implemented as "the Congress governments do exactly the opposite of what they profess."[6]

The Samaj organized "patrol squads" in the 200 villages of Surat district "to keep a vigil." Each squad was headed by a "Commander" for a group of ten villages. It also organized "Sardar Senas" to protect the crops in the region. On November 24, 1973, a meeting of landless labourers was interrupted at Bardoli, south Gujarat, by the young sons of farmers. A Harijan youth was injured in stone-throwing.[7] Similar incidents also took place in some villages of central Gujarat.[8]

During the first week of December, the citizens of Rajkot city, Saurashtra, organized demonstrations demanding water for the city from the Bhadar Dam. At the same time, the farmers of Rajkot district threatened the government that they would launch a three-stage agitation, culminating in a satyagraha in the final stage, to forcibly release irrigation water from Bhadar Dam to the standing sugarcane and cotton crop in an area of 7,000 acres in Rajkot district. The government released the water immediately.

Another major issue on which the peasants defied the government in December was that of levy. (The paddy levy is, in fact, not new. It was introduced by the ruler of the erstwhile Baroda State.) The government has made several changes in the Levy Act over the years. The 1973 Levy Act is an improvement over the 1967 Act. First, small farmers having one acre or less were exempted from the levy. Secondly, the levy was progressive so that big farmers had to give a larger share than small farmers. The idea was that only those farmers who were rich and had benefited from planned development were to be affected. Thus, in Surat district, out of 70,000 farmers only 27,000 farmers (i.e. 39 per cent) had to pay levy at differential rates.[9] But as on previous occasions, the big farmers mobilized all peasants against the levy in the name of the common interest of the sons of the soil. We shall return to this point later when we discuss the agitation.

URBAN LABOURERS

The poor, casual and unskilled labourers are generally dumb. In the villages from where they migrate to urban areas they are landless labourers hardly getting enough work to keep themselves alive. As a rule, they are illiterate. In urban areas, they live in slums, and their belongings are meagre; they live at a sub-human level. The present political system is completely alien to them. They are the most vulnerable to high prices and scarcity. But this is nothing new to them. Even during normal times, prices have been always beyond their reach, making it impossible for them to meet even their essential needs which are anyway very few.

Factory labourers are of two types. First there are those who work on a daily wage basis. The factory act and rules do not apply to them. If they work for longer hours and produce more, they get more money. They do not get wages for Sundays and other holidays when they do not work. They are unorganized.

The other type of factory labourers are those organized in trade unions. Most of these trade unions in Gujarat are dominated by the Majoor Mahajan which is wedded to the philosophy of class collaboration and not class conflict. The Mahajan avoids direct action such as strikes or gheraos. Even during the large-scale retrenchment of workers in the textile mills in 1972, the Mahajan did not launch any agitation. However, a few trade unions are controlled by socialist and communist parties. Barring a few exceptions, all the trade unions, by and large, work as brokers between the management and the workers. Or they work as clearing agencies for taking the problems to the labour officers and other authorities. Once in a while they negotiate with the management on issues such as bonus or rise in wages. But they do not aim at developing a working class consciousness among the factory workers. Consequently, the factory workers look upon their problems in terms of economic demands and are not concerned with the larger issues relating to the societal structure. As a result, fraternity among the workers as a class has not developed in Gujarat. In fact, they have remained quite divided—among Hindus, Baniyas, Harijans, Muslims and so on. During the 1969 communal riots some of these workers killed each other.[10]

AGRICULTURE LABOURERS

The number of agricultural labourers has risen in Gujarat at an alarming rate during the last decade from 14.77 per cent of the working population in 1961 to 22.48 per cent in 1971. A few of them are attached labourers who are employed either on annual contracts, i.e., from Holi to Holi (April to March), or on seasonal contracts for four months. As attached labourers, they live with the employer and perform all sorts of chores from cleaning utensils to tilling the land. They are not organized, and in social and political matters they follow the instructions of their masters. A large number of agricultural labourers are casual workers. They get employment for about 7 months in a year. For the remaining period, they either do not have anything to do or migrate to urban areas in search of unskilled jobs or work on their own land, if they have any. It is estimated that on an average a labourer is totally unemployed for a period of 100 days in a year. He gets roughly from Rs.1 to Rs.3 per day for agricultural work. Seasonal employment and meagre income make the agricultural labourers' life extremely difficult. Except in south Gujarat, they are unorganized; therefore, their participation in any protest activity is negligible.

In south Gujarat, Sarvodaya workers have organized agricultural labourers, particularly the Dublas or Halpatis. The Halpati Seva Sangh, an organization of agricultural labourers, works on the philosophy of class collaboration. The workers of the Sangh preach harmony between landlords and labourers. It mainly conducts welfare activities such as constructing huts, conducting night schools, and propagating prohibition to uplift the labourers. The landlords, however, do not approve of these reformist activities of the Gandhians; they fear that education and consciousness among the Halpatis would endanger their interests; and therefore they try to curb the activities of the Sangh. This obviously creates conflicts between the landlords and Halpatis—as, for instance, in 1973, when the Halpatis of some villages launched a strike against landlords demanding a daily wage of Rs.3. In such situations, interestingly

enough, the Gandhian workers pacify and control the
labourers. As Jan Breman observes, "The social workers
intervene in order to prevent rising tensions and to reach a
compromise. Self-respect and class consciousness are not taught.
On the contrary, the organization does not aim at making the
Halpatis able to stand up for themselves, aware of their exploitation and oppression, but envisages their adjustment to the
social system without a fundamental change in their dependence"[11].

MIDDLE CLASS

The middle class consists of the upward mobile sections of
intermediary and higher castes engaged in white-collar jobs or
small business. Like the working class, there is no common
interest or ideology that inspires this class. It is divided into
several group of interests. Income-wise, the lower middle class —
clerks, typists, accountants, shop assistants, teachers, petty
shop-keepers, etc.—is not better off than the industrial workers.
Yet a great social gap divides the two; they live in different
residential areas in the cities. Industrial workers live in slums
and chawls where the economic condition of the people is by
and large the same. Persons of lower middle class live in *poles*,
i.e., streets, or recently constructed housing societies outside
the old residential towns where the upper middle class and the
rich also live. Thus their aspirations, norms and values are
those of the rich. For instance, a clerk desires to have a
refrigerator, a fan, a sofa-set, etc., because his neighbour or his
relative possesses these things. For him, these are status
symbols. But he does not have the means to have all these
'luxury' items (looked upon by his class as necessities) which
the neighbour who is either a government officer or a small
factory-owner has as a matter of course. Consequently, the
present economic hardship hits him hard. The sense of "relative
deprivation" is very strong in him.

A middle class person is generally vocal and sensitive. He
gets angry when he does not get a bus in time He quarrels
with the bus conductor, the rickshaw-driver, the station master,
the postmaster, even the policeman and the government officer.
He fights with shopkeepers and hawkers when they raise prices

or indulge in fraudulent measurements or adulteration. He feels that it is his right to fight against injustice. And he finds injustice everywhere. "All are corrupt" he exclaims. But he finds himself helpless against government servants, organized bus conductors, rickshaw drivers, traders, police, etc. He sees immorality all around him. But he does not organize as a class against other organized interests. This is why consumer movements of the middle class have not succeeded against traders and farmers.

He feels that in the present social structure he suffers the most. He complains against the government, against its schemes for the development of backward classes and against welfare programmes for the labourers. He also complains against industrialists and big businessmen. He feels somewhat like this : "Poor persons do not have many needs, and they do not have to observe a certain life style... Rich persons have no problems. But we of the middle class have short means and long demands concerning the life style; we have to maintain our status. A poor person can beg, but we cannot. We are, therefore, sandwiched between the affluent and the poor." The most organized and articulate sections of the middle class are the teachers and the students, both large in numbers and highly sensitive and vocal.

TEACHERS

College teachers, who mainly belong to the upper and middle castes, are a force to reckon with in Gujarat. During the last decade they have organized and developed a powerful teachers' organization for protecting and advancing their interests against university and college managements, largely dominated by big businessmen, industrialists and rich peasants.

Further, college teachers of Gujarat in general, and of Ahmedabad in particular, are more politicized than many other sections of the middle class. Some of the college teachers write regularly in the vernacular newspapers on all major issues facing society. College teachers in general, and their organizational leaders in particular, were against Chimanbhai Patel who had been a teacher, a principal of a college, and a manager over a string of colleges. Chimanbhai Patel had used his control over the colleges for political ends. He was responsible for bringing back Ishvarbhai Patel as Vice-Chancellor of Gujarat University. Ishvarbhai Patel had earlier been bitterly opposed by college teachers and made to resign. It may be noted that despite their strength and organization, college teachers could not succeed in the elections to the University Executive (Syndicate) and in the Vice-Chancellor's election in which Chiman Patel, using his power and patronage as Chief Minister, had personally and openly canvassed for his own candidates. The teachers' leaders had launched an agitation for preventing Chiman Patel from becoming the Chief Minister in 1973.[12] Both the political success of Chiman Patel and his success in imposing his will on the affairs of the University produced a sharp sense of frustration among teachers.

STUDENTS

As elsewhere, more then 75 per cent of undergraduate students come from middle-income or high-income groups and belong to high or middle castes. The composition of the students, by their father's occupations, varies from city college to taluka town colleges. In the cities, according to a survey of college students, the father's of 36 per cent of the students are white-collar employees either in government or in private service. The fathers of about 27 per cent of the students are either businessmen or factory owners. And 16 per cent of the students are sons of farmers. Barely 2 per cent of the students come from the working class[13]. In taluka town colleges a majority of the students are sons and daughters of farmers. Among the hostel students of Baroda, Ahmedabad, Surat, Morvi, Bhavnagar and Rajkot, many belong to the landed class.

A large number of students are not interested in their studiess. They find their studies tiresome, boring, bearing little relationship to their lives. The students, particularly those belonging to the lower middle class, complain that the present education does not enable them to earn a stable livelihood. They constantly worry about their future economic security. But they do not know the way out. They therefore imitate the rich students. Students belonging to families of rich peasants, factory owners and big businessmen do not care for their studies either-though for quite different reasons. For them college life is a picnic. They say, "We do not care for studies; we do not want degrees. We have enough land... We have joined college just to have the experience of college life. This is the time to enjoy life." On the whole, except for their dress and permissiveness in sex relationships, available studies suggest, students do not hold values different from their parents or the ruling class.[14]

However, a small but significant section of students in all cities is more sensitive to social problems such as poverty, inequality and injustice. For instance, a group of students in Ahmedabad formed a group, name *Hun*, i.e., "I", in 1971. In 1972, the group brought out a mimeographed booklet, 'Donkey', in which it satirically compared politicians with donkeys. On January 26, 1973, the group published a booklet '*Bhukh*', i.e., hunger. On the front page it says, "What are '*ladus*' ? Where are the '*ladus*' ? Are those '*ladus*' meant to be thrown away ? Are they to be worn ? Or, are they to be eaten ?" The point that the group was making was that poor people do not know what '*ladus*' are. Significantly, the booklet was inaugurated by a shoe-shine boy. In Baroda and Surat, some students organized study circles in 1973 to discuss economic and political problems. A few students also sometimes visit slum areas with a view to helping the poor.

The more affluent section of the student community is not serious about its studies. They either read during the last month before the examination or get marks through underhand means. Many of them are more interested in films than in sports, debates, drama, dance or discussion. They roam about on the college campus, tease girls, use vituperative language, sit in restaurants, go to film show, take LSD or liquor and thus simply 'kill' time. When in a crowd, they harass the older men, bus drivers, conductors, hotel boys, hawkers and above all, girls. They have a nuisance value in urban areas. Their mischief and supposedly carefree life attract many other students to their fold. And with money they are able to collect groups around them. They are always in favour of a strike if for no reason than fun.

There is no powerful city or state level students' organization except the Akhil Bhartiya Vidyarthi Parishad, which is associated with the Jana Sangh. During the last five years, about a dozen student organizations have come into existence in Ahmedabad. But none of them has a stable network, programme or regular membership. They are largely *ad hoc* creations of some temporary events. They launch agitations and issue statements, but there is no follow-up action. Most of these organizations are supported by different political leaders belonging to the ruling as well as opposition parties. In order to make their appeal citywide, the various organizations get united under some common banner. For instance, the Vidyarthi Madhyastha Samiti was formed in 1971 for launching an agitation against the fee-rise in Ahmedabad.

Student agitations have become endemic in India since 1966-67. During the period 1967-68 to 1969-70, the incidence of agitation among university students on a rough count was around 45 agitations per 10,000 students per year; and of these around 14 per cent were violent. Large-scale student agitations had become a regular feature after 1965.[15] We do not have data on student agitations for the whole of Gujarat. However, the data on protest and violent incidents in Surat and Ahmedabad suggest that Gujarat was relatively peaceful till 1963; the number of student protests has increased in the last five years.

Our own survey data on the students of Surat city suggest that most students participated in school or college strikes. About 49 per cent of the undergraduate (Arts and Commerce) students approved of strikes in colleges on student problems. They believed that teachers and college authorities did not listen to their complaints. Thirty-four per cent of the students, however, disapproved of strikes. They felt that only rowdy students organized strikes. Some of them were of the view that most of the strikes were organized on flimsy grounds.

During 1973, the students of Gujarat launched several agitations. In March-April, B. Com. students walked out of the examination halls in Ahmedabad in protest against 'tough' question papers. The authorities gave in to their demand for a re-examination in all papers. In June-July, students of the Ayurvedic College of Ahmedabad damaged the college building. In July, students launched an agitation protesting against the in-fighting in the Congress party between the Chiman Patel and the Oza factions. They also gave a call for bandh in support of their demands. In October, students of the H.L. Commerce College, Ahmedabad, demanded the postponement of first-term tests as they wanted to participate in flood relief work. The college authorities and teachers did not listen to the students' demand and the principal and the professors resigned *en bloc* in protest against the demands. The students had to withdraw the demand, but tension continued.

In November 1973, students of Petlad College of Kheda district organized a procession demanding the reinstatement of the principal of the college. All colleges of the district supported the demand.

In Baroda, the conflict between students and the State Transport Authority was a permanent feature throughout 1974. In south Gujarat, students launched an agitation against fee-rise and for the removal of the "internal evaluation" system. In Surat, Navsari and Chikhli, several incidents of student unrest were reported. In Saurashtra, particularly in Bhavnagar, Morvi, Rajkot and Jamnagar, student agitations on some issue or the other had been reported almost every other month in the newspapers.

As a result of the new University Act, the students of Gujarat University were given representation, and 11 out of 145 seats in the University Court (Senate) were allotted to them. In October 1973, in the elections to the Court, students were mobilized by teachers, political parties and managements. Because of their resources, the managements won over the students' support for their nominees in the elections. Some popular teachers and students were defeated. This produced frustration among the student leaders.

3. CHANGES IN THE STYLE OF POLITICS

With the formation of Gujarat state in 1960 and the introduction of Panchayati Raj in 1963, public life of Gujarat entered a new phase in its political style—a gradual progression from elitist to mass politics. Till the mid-1960s the Baniya-Brahman style of politics had dominated with its vague Gandhian concepts of propriety in public life. This style was largely acceptable to the urban educated middle class, particularly the upper castes engaged in white-collar jobs or business. In this style, an individual's personal and public life are so divided that while any means that leads to success is acceptable in private life, 'purity' in public life is to be insisted upon. The latter implies two things. One, there should not be coercion and corruption in public life either to win over or to defeat one's opponents. Accommodation of both followers and opponents in the distribution of positions or favours, with a view to maintaining oneself in power, was acceptable. But the use of either money or intimidation or the recourse to coercive methods was not acceptable and was considered both undemocratic and bad. Second, the dealings with finances of public institutions should always be above suspicion. One can cite several examples of businessmen accumulating money through illegitimate means, but in their association with public institutions they are straightforward and meticulous in maintaining accounts, etc.

There has been another style of politics alongside this, with accent on success by any means. In this style, the end is more important than the means, and one is free to adopt any means to attain and maintain political power. There is no inhibition against distribution of money, use of coercion, kidnapping and intimidation. These are accepted as an inevitable part of politics.

The Gujarat Congress was dominated by the Baniya-Brahmin style of politics till the formation of a separate state of Gujarat in 1960. It was one of the most disciplined, well-knit and organized political parties in the country. Though there were groups within the party, these had not as sharply crystalized as in many of the northern states. The state party was outside the factional structure that was conceived as an integral part of the "Congress system". Most of the decisions of the party were taken by consensus. The leader, who dominated the organization, was expected to be above all groups. Congressmen believed that the party was like a 'family', and that therefore party difference should not be discussed outside the party. Almost till 1967, the Gujarat Congress by and large did not take its internal problems to the Congress High Command for resolution. The working of this style was evident even during the Jivaraj Mehta episode in 1963.

At the same time, the Jivaraj Mehta episode was the begin-

ning of the decline of the Baniya-Brahmin style of politics.
Chimanbhai Patel, Kantilal Ghiya, and Thakorbhai Desai
took a lead in organizing a signature compaign against
Mehta on the ground that he had not accepted the
directive of the *movadi*, i.e., the elderly leader (Morarji Desai).[16]
Morarji disapproved of the move because he believed that a
signature compaign against an elected leader was not a healthy
practice, and yet he took the responsibility on his shoulders,
as befitted a *movadi*. This was the Baniya-Brahmin style.
However, the point should be underlined that the urban middle
class did not approve of the way in which Jivaraj Mehta was
ousted.

By the beginning of the 1960s, Patidar and Kshatriya groups
in the Swatantra party joined hands to break the monolithic
structure of the Congress. Both of them have a feudal past,
and they had little respect for the Gandhian style of politics.
They followed the manipulative style both within and outside
the Swatantra party. In 1967-68, the Swatantra party having
failed to capture power, adopted this style in an even more
naked form. Its leaders resorted to means which included
coercion, bribery, and kidnapping of MLAs to win over the
members of the Congress.[17] Although this style of politics had
been prevalent in the villages, it was for the first time that it
was practised openly and on a large scale in Ahmedabad, the
state capital. Reacting to this and in order to preserve itself
in power, the Congress party followed the same style. But
because of its well-knit organization, it did not have to adopt
it as openly as the Swatantra party.

The hold of the Swatantra party declined with the split in
the Congress in 1969. The new Congress followed the manipulative style of politics, and emerged as a strong party in the
state after the 1972 state assembly elections. Ghanshyam Oza
became the Chief Minister of Gujarat in March 1972. Faction
fights began within the party. Both the Oza-Adani-Darji
group and the Chimanbhai-Ghiya group followed the manipulative style of politics. But Patel proved more skillful than
the others and managed to edge them out. By now the Baniya-
Brahmin style of politics had become obsolete. And during
the last three years, popular vernacular newspapers have
reported in detail the day-to-day manipulations in politics.

The conscious and vocal sections of society, particularly the urban middle classes, became disgusted with politics. They branded it as "corrupt politics" and revolted againt it.

The politicians began to rely so much on manipulative politics that they lost their contact with the masses. In the cities as well as in the villages, the party leaders increasingly depended on brokers, smugglers, goondas and those who provided finance to the party rather than on committed party cadre. The old guard, who were respected and who were always ready to help the people, have slowly disappeared from the scene. Professional politicians, who are not respected or liked, had taken over. People go to politicians for getting certain concessions from the government, and politicians approach the people for votes during the elections. These politicians have no moral authority nor any influence over the people.

THE POLITICAL PARTIES

The character of the ruling Congress, except for increased exhortations in favour of socialism, has remained the same as and was the undivided Congress. It is a hotchpotch of various divergent interests. In order to win the 1971 and 1972 elections, the party obtained the support of smugglers, bootleggers, as well as rich peasants, factory-owners and businessmen. It got men, money and material from these groups, but made promises to the middle class, the poor and the labourers. All shades of opinion and opinion holders, from Swatantra to Communist, were accomodated in the Congress.

However, the party has certain disadvantages as compared to the undivided Congress. First, the new Congress in Gujarat was born out of manipulative politics. Some joined the party because certain opportunities were offered to them. Some joined it because they had no opportunities in the undivided Congress. And some others joined it because they realised this party was sure to assume power after the 1971 elections. Only a few joined the new Congress on ideological grounds. Consequently, there was more opportunism than party commitment among Congressmen. They were more interested in attaining personal power than in building up the party. Secondly, though there were conflicts and factions in the undivided Congress, the faction fights in the ruling party were very sharp and open. During the last two years, many of the state level leaders had undermined the party's prestige and discipline.

Most of the state-level party leaders were deeply involved in internal power struggles, and they had no interest in building up the party. The Central High Command of the party entrusted the responsibility for party building to Jinabhai Darji. He was made the convenor in April 1972 after the state Assembly elections. Darji, an artisan by caste, rural bred, who had worked among the tribals for many years, had sympathy for the poor. He did not have the sophistication of the middle classes or the rich. When he was the president of the district panchayat for more than five years, he dealt firmly with officials. He has a harsh tongue. Because of his pro-poor policies and harsh tongue he was rather unpopular among the urban middle class. The upper middle class, rich peasants and businessmen were bitterly against him. Most of the vernacular Press started a campaign against Darji after he became the president of the Gujarat Congress. However, the youth, who had joined the party with the hope of bringing about socialism, and the backward classes enthusiastically supported Darji. They puined their hope on him.

After becoming the convenor Darji travelled all over the state to organize the party. He also tried to mobilize young persons. At the same time, he firmly dealt with opportunistic elements and tried to keep businessmen and blackmarketeers out of the party. He won the election to the Gujarat Congress presidentship against Vakharia, an ex-PSP member and a nominee of Chiman Patel. Ex-communists like Himmatsinh and others joined hands with Patel against Darji. Despite his victory, presidentship was not smooth sailing for Darji. His opponents were bitterly against him and missed no opportunity to embarrass him. At the same time, many of his supporters who, though they had backed him against Chiman Patel for different reasons, did not support his pro-poor politics and his party-building activity. Consequently, Darji had willy-nilly to struggle both within and outside his group. Most of his time was spent in solving disputes among different groups. As a result, offices party could not be organized at several taluka places. And there is evidence to show that even some district offices were not functioning and remained closed for weeks. Taluka and district leaders were busy pulling each other down Darji did not get the co-operation of state and district party bosses, and he did not have funds even to run the state party office. He frequently expressed his desire to the High Command to resign from the post.

On the government front, the party's record was poor. Soon after the Congress came to power, the state faced a serious drought. Despite this, the government under Oza managed to perform rather well initially. But slowly, the government was losing its grip over the economic problems which worsened after the change of chief ministers and the preoccupation of the opposing factions with day-to-day political wrangling. The prices of some essential commodities rose very high in July 1973. The government was helpless. The rich peasants and big businessmen who had financed the party began to assert their claims.

In July 1973, Oza was ousted by Patel through manipulative politics. Patel got the support of the communists as well as industrialists in his bid to capture power. He passed certain legislations which looked socialist; but when it came to implementing these measures, he and the administration succumbed to pressures from rich peasants and big businessmen. Consequently the poor people both in the cities and in the countryside were alienated.

Chiman Patel became Chief Minister at a time when food riots had started in Ahmedabad. In order to contain the riot situation and to win popularity, Patel announced several measures aimed at controlling prices. Narendrasinh Jhala, the Minister for Civic Supply, once a Swatantra party leader, announced in August that several businessmen had agreed to reduce the prices of commodities used by the urban middle class. However, Jhala's agreement with the businessmen did not work for even a fortnight: prices increased further after August. Both Jhala and Patel repeatedly announced that the government would take action against hoarders and blackmarketeers. In December, the Chief Minister announced a series of measures, including invocation of the DIR, to deal with hoarders in the state. Export of foodgrains like wheat, rice, paddy and bajra from the state was banned. But all these remained mere announcements. They were not followed up by any action. Jhala publicly accepted that their threats had no impact on rich farmers or traders.

The moral authority of the government had by now been seriously eroded. People felt that the government was not capable of controlling prices. The Patel government, according to them, did not mean business. Such feelings were reflected in news items, editorials, articles and letters in the newspapers. Further, rumours spread in the cities that Chimanbhai and Jhala had taken several lakhs of rupees from businessmen and oil dealers and that in turn, they had allowed the prices of edible oil to rise steeply despite a bumper crop. Some ministers were known to maintain open contacts with known smugglers and black-marketeers. All this raised doubts in the minds of the people about the sincerity of the ministry. There were also strong rumours that Patel and Chhabil Mehta, the Public Works Minister in Patel's cabinet, took money even from government servants for withdrawing corruption cases. Several other similar rumours gained currency. What is important to note here is that such rumours, none of which was effectively countered, created hostility against the Chief Minister. For the first time, corruption charges had been levelled against the Chief Minister in public. And Chiman Patel lost credibility in the public eye rather quickly.

Thus, both on the organization and government fronts, the Congress party's record of performance was poor. The gulf between the people—particularly the disorganized middle class—and the party increased. Within the party, some of the so-called radicals felt that the Chief Minister was siding with rich peasants and the black-marketeers. They also felt that he was depending solely on corrupt tactics. But they were in a minority in the party and therefore helpless. Consequently, directly or indirectly, some of the top leaders supported the students' agitation. We shall return to this point again. Suffice it to note here that the Congress was a divided house. And factions were based on personal considerations and not on ideology.

OPPOSITION PARTIES

The Congress (O) in Gujarat had been reduced in strength after the 1972 Assembly elections. Many left the party and those who remained were frustrated The party became almost dormant for a year. However, thanks to the strong party loyalty among members, the party slowly recovered from its shock aud launched certain programmes in 1973. A team of party volunteers worked in the drought-affected areas and organized campaigns against price rise in mid-1973. The party organized a torch march throughout the state for rousing public opinion on the Narmada issue. It also organized a training camp for those who were to launch a satyagraha for securing a height of 560 feet for the proposed Narmada dam. The party also supported the anti-levy movement launched by the peasants and thus tried to get rehabilitated among them. People began to compare the Patel ministry with Hitendra Desai ministry of the undivided Congress and felt that the latter had been at least not corrupt.

The Jana Sangh too slowly gained ground in the urban areas. Its nationalist posture and militancy attracted young boys The party took up local issues and launched agitations. For instance, during the first week of December 1973, the party organized a large-scale agitation on the water problem in Rajkot. The demonstration was followed by looting and arson. Like Congress (O), Jana Sangh supported the anti-levy movement of the peasants and also launched a campaign against rising prices.

However, though the Congress (O) and the Jana Sangh could rouse opinion among the urban people against price rise, they could not attract large masses to their party activities. Their meetings and processions consisted of not more than a few hundred persons in Ahmedabad, Baroda or Surat. The Leftist parties, CPI and CPM, have very little influence in Gujarat.

4. CONCLUSION

Since the beginning of the seventies, hopes among the urban and rural poor in Gujarat had been aroused. On the other hand, big businessmen and rich peasants became alarmed by the 'garibi hatao' slogan of the Congress. They organized themselves and pressurized the government to look after their interests. The party in power, dominated by the rich, succumbed to their pressures, both at the policy and the implementation levels. Artificial scarcity, black-marketing and rising prices were the result.

The Congress party remained a crowd of opportunists. A few young idealists found themselves misfits in the party; they therefore left it in disgust. Party bosses at all levels were involved in cutting each other's throat. Industrialists, big businessmen and rich peasants worked hand in hand with political leaders of different parties. The educated urban middle class, were put off by the manipulative politics of the Congress. But they did not find any alternative party to support. The average urban dweller found himself powerless and alienated. His faith in the present political system had been shaken during the previous two years. An increasing number of all people found violence and direct action to be inevitable to solve their problems. With this background, we shall now turn to the agitation.

NOTES

1. *Census of India* 1971, *Gujarat Town Directory, Part VIA*, Delhi, the Manager of Publications, 1972.
2. 187 persons selected at random from 19 blocks, were interviewed with a structured questionnaire. Besides, 100 persons were also interviewed in depth on talking points.
3. *Gujarat Samachar*, (Ahmedabad), November 21, 1973.
4. *Gujarat Samachar*, December 18, 1973.
5. *Times of India* (Ahmedabad), November 13 and 15, 1973.
6. *Gujrat Mitra* (Surat), November 25, 1973.
7. *Ibid.*
8. *Gujarat Samachar*, November 20, 1973.
9. Pramod Mehta, "Opposition Adopts Double Standards" *Indian Express* (Ahmedabad), January 9, 1974.
10. Ghanshyam Shah, Communal Riots in Gujarat, *Economic And Political Weekly*, Annual Number, Vol. V, Nos. 3, 4 and 5, January 1970.
11. "Mobilisation of Landless Lobourers : Halpatis of South Gujarat", *Economic and Political Weekly*, Vol. IX, No. 12, March 23, 1974.
12. Ghanshyam Shah, "Anatomy of Urban Riots : Ahmedabad 1973", *Economic And Political Weekly*, Vol. IX, Nos. 6, 7 and 8, Annual

Number, February 1974.

13. Centre for Regional Development Studies, Surat and National Service Scheme, K.P. College of Commerce, Surat, carried out a survey of undergraduate students of Arts and Commerce. We interviewed 224 students in November-December 1973.

14. The findings are based on the above study. See also K D. Gangrade, "Inter-generational Difference : A Study in the Generation Gap", (mimeographed; Delhi School of Social Work, 1974) and B.V. Shah, *Social Change And College Students of Gujarat*, Baroda, the M.S. University of Baroda, 1964.

15. K.C. Pant, "Violence in a Period of Social Change", *Young India*, Vol. 3, Nos. 29 and 30, 1973.

16. Ghanshyam Shah, "Sarvocha Neta : Gujarat Congress" *Vishvamanav* (Gujarati), May 1968.

17. Ghanshyam Shah, *Caste Association and Political Process in Gujarat*, Bombay, Popular Prakashan, 1975.

2

The Agitation : Unorganized Masses and Organized Groups

We have already provided the background to the events that rocked Gujarat from January to March 1974. We shall now give an account of the agitation.

1. AGITATIONS

In July 1973, on the eve of the change of the Chief Minister, from Ghanshyam Oza to Chiman Patel, the teachers and students of Ahmedabad launched an agitation against corrupt politics. The agitation turned into food riots and then communal riots. The police, however, controlled the situation within three days.[1] The law and order situation returned to normalcy quickly. But tension continued; in fact it was steadily mounting, expressing itself in sporadic riots at several places in the state. The January-March agitation was a continuation of the prevailing tension in the state. The riots and agitations were all directed against the government. Some of these took place simultaneously and it is therefore difficult to give a precise chronological account At the same time, there seems to have been a certain sequence of developments. The objectives of the agitation seem to have changed in a certain order.

ANTI-PRICE RISE AGITATION

As discussed earlier, the food problem became acute in December 1973. People found it extremely difficult in the face of constantly raising prices. Several voluntary organizations such as locality organizations, youth clubs, women's organizations and other non-political organizations, as well as political parties, raised their voice against the price rise and scarcity of foodgrains. The problem also boldly featured in newspaper headlines.

Some organizations clamoured for a state-wide agitation against high prices. The Civil Supplies Minister publicly admitted that the food position was not satisfactory in Gujarat. He alleged that the Centre was not supplying adequate quota of foodgrains to the state. The Chief Minister also said the state would face a crisis on the food front in the following months. Contradictory statements by different ministers appeared in the Press on food supply and distribution pattern. One of the top ranking leaders of the Congress party asked for the resignation of the Civil Supplies Minister for his failure to meet the needs of the people. One MLA from south Gujarat threatened to resign if the government failed to control prices and provide foodgrains to the masses. Some dissident Congress leaders called a meeting of partymen on January 5, 1974 to discuss the launching of an agitation against scarcity and price rise. A Congress MLA said in public that the Chief Minister was protecting vested interests. He alleged that ministers were indulging in corrupt practices in broad daylight. He, along with 23 other MLAs, demanded President's rule in the state for a period of six months. However, the people did not place much trust in their radical speeches. They believed that such speeches were only part of the power struggle in the Congress. They asserted that they wanted foodgrains and not speeches.

Congress (O) declared in the last week of December that the party would organize meetings in various areas to mobilize public opinion against price rise. A conference of the Gujarat Chamber of Commerce held in Ahmedabad on January 5 demanded denationalization of wholesale wheat trade. It alleged that the food crisis in the country was due to the nationalization of wheat trade.

The Jana Sangh was very active in Ahmedabad and Saurashtra in exploiting the grievances of the masses. It gave a call to observe an anti-price rise week in Ahmedabad and elsewhere. On January 1, 1974 it gave a call for Jetpur (in Saurashtra) bandh. The party organized a procession and attempted to lock the Mamlatdar's office. The police foiled the attempt. The agitators retaliated against the police action by throwing stones. Later, the crowd looted two shops and set fire to the purchase and sale shop from where foodgrains were distributed. Lathi-charge and tear-gassing followed. 175 men and women courted arrest, and the police arrested another 80 persons on charge of looting. The Jana Sangh again gave a call for Jetpur bandh on the following day as a protest against alleged police atrocities in the town.

In Ahmedabad, the Jana Sangh organized public meetings every day from January 1 against the price rise. Stone-throwing incidents invariably marked the end of every meeting. On January 6, stone-throwing took place in as many as seven places in Ahmedabad. The places were middle class localities, viz. Khadia, Dariapur, Relief Road, Gandhi Road, Delhi Chakla, Saraspur and Kalupur. These localities were to become the storm centres in the subsequent agitation. Lathi-charge, tear-gas and, at one place, firing also took place.

ANTI-LEVY SATYAGRAHA

While the anti-price rise agitation was spreading in urban Gujarat, a different kind of agitation developed in the rural areas of south Gujarat. This was the anti-levy satyagraha. In order to show the importance and strength of the farmers, the Khedut Samaj stopped the supply of milk and vegetables to the cities for two days. The government, having a soft corner for the peasants, did not take any firm action against the agitators. In fact, landless labourers declared that they would assist the government in collecing the levy. They also said that they would show the godowns of the farmers to the officers for procurement. In retaliation against this offer and following the arrest of Khedut Samaj leaders, disturbances took place in Bardoli on January 3. The young sons of farmers were active in the anti-levy satyagraha. They were more militant than their fathers. They organized a procession in protest against the arrest of two Khedut Samaj leaders. A crowd of students attacked Arvind Desai, a prominent leader of landless labourers and at that time a close associate of Jhinabhai Darji, the GPCC President. He was severely beaten and his house and furniture were set on fire.

After this, confrontation took place between landless labourers and farmers in that village in Surat district.

On the following day, January 4, a procession of three to four hundred persons, mainly diamond cutters who were migrants from Saurashtra and were known for their rough ways, was organized in Surat. It turned unruly and the crowd went on a rampage and forced the traders of the city to close their shops. Stones were thrown at public and private property. Incidents of looting and arson also took place. "Khedut Samaj Zindabad" and "Indira Murdabad" were the two slogans shouted by the crowd. Significantly, there were no slogans against Chiman Patel or the Gujarat government. On inquiry, we came across several people who were more concerned with price-rise than with the cause of the Khedut Samaj but who had joined the agitation because it was against the government. It was not a spontaneous demonstration, the procession was organized and supported by some political leaders of Surat city.

On the 7th, a bandh was observed in several south Gujarat towns (Valsad, Bardoli, Valod, Buhari, Navsari, etc.) which are the strongholds of the peasants—again, in protest against the arrest of the Khedut Samaj leaders.

STUDENTS

The rise in prices had affected hostel students. In December, the mess bill rose from Rs. 85 to Rs. 120. According to the manager of the mess of L.D. Engineering College in Ahmedabad, about 45 to 50 per cent of the students found it difficult to pay the mess bill regularly. The hostel inmates were also dissatisfied with the quality of food, as one of them (a final year student from Morvi) said, "This is not a new problem for us. Ever since I joined the college, we have been complaining against the quality of food and sometimes we boycott our lunch or dinner." Besides food and bad management of the mess, the student anger was aroused by the internal evaluation system, the semester system, the authoritarian attitude of teachers etc.

On the issues of the mess bill, the students of L.D. Engineering College became violent, setting fire to the furniture and other belongings of the rector on December 20, 1973. The rector resigned and a committee was formed to look into the demands of the students. Similarly, on December 28, 1973 after returning from a party given by a Jana Sangh leader who had been elected to the municipality, about 150 students of Morvi Engineering College destroyed the furniture of the college and the mess. They beat up one of the two rectors and his son; the furniture and a scooter were set ablaze. The agitation continued for four days. The college was closed.

The agitated students of L. D. Engineering College of Ahmedabad again went on a strike on January 3, 1974 on the same issue. The students destroyed college and hostel furniture. Police entered the campus and the confrontation between students and police continued for several hours on the 3rd and the 4th. Some students were severely beaten up by the police, some were arrested; and it was alleged by several students that policemen stole their wrist watches and money. The behaviour of the police added fuel to the fire.

The Engineering College being situated in the vicinity of the university campus, the incident affected the students of other colleges and hostels. On the 5th, about 1,000 students went to Navrangpura police station in a procession, demanding the release of the arrested students of the hostel. The police constable in charge of the police station expressed his inability to comply with the demand as it was beyond his power to take a decision. The infuriated mob went to the Congress House. There they asked the Congress Secretary to convey their feelings to the Chief Minister and the Congress President. The President was out of station and the Chief Minister said that he did not have time to meet the students. The students discovered that the Chief Minister had time to attend the premier show of a film. They felt that the government did not care for the people. Consequently for the first time anti-Chiman Patel slogans began to be raised. However, the Police Commissioner later met the students and released the arrested students who numbered more than three hundred. Following the agitation of the students of the engineering colleges of Ahmedabad and Morvi, some students of Ahmedabad formed a committee called the Yuvak Lagni (feeling) Samiti. The Samiti gave a call for an indefinite strike in schools and colleges from January 7 to protest against the closure of the L.D. Engineering College, and the increased mess charges in the hostels. Most of the school and college students responded to the call. Sporadic incidents of stone-throwing took place on Relief Road and Gandhi Road.

A meeting of more than a hundred student representatives of different colleges was held at Sardarbag on January 7. The meeting endorsed the call for a strike and directed that the strike should continue. The major demands of the Yuvak Lagni Samiti were reduction of mess bills and redressal of certain educational grievances. They were :

(1) mess bills of hostels should not exceed Rs. 70 per month, per student;
(2) police atrocity should end;
(3) the university should reduce term fees by Rs. 10;
(4) the conveners of the Youth Festivals must resign because they invited hoarders, businessmen and black-marketeers instead of artists and educationists at the valedictory session;
(5) the Education Minister should resign as she did not carry out her duties;
(6) police should not enter the university campus;
(7) the university should stop compulsory collection of Rs. 2 for mark-sheets; and,
(8) hoarders and profiteers should be arrested and quality foodgrains should be distributed to the masses.

Besides several college-based student organizations, the Akhil Bharatiya Vidyarthi Parishad, the student front of the Jana Sangh, supported the demands of the Lagni Samiti. The members of the Vidyarthi Parishad observed fast on the pavement near Apna Bazar, a co-operative store. Thus, it was an attempt to link the students' problem with the anti-price rise agitation of the Jana Sangh. Soon after the Sardarbag meeting, a student mob damaged the car of the Finance Minister, Amul Desai.

During the night a number of shops selling foodgrains, provisions, oil and ghee were looted by the mob. The worst affected areas were Khadiya, Saraspur, Dhana Sutharni Pole, Vadigam, Dariapur, Panch Bhai Pole and Chhaga Bari. In a clash between students and police, six policemen and several students were injured. The police arrested 188 persons.

In Saurashtra several towns, Dharangadhra, Gondal,

Jasadan, Jamnagar, etc., also observed bandh on the 7th in response to the Jana Sangh's call. In Dharangadhra a clash between police and the crowd continued for three hours. The police resorted to lathi--charge and also burst tear-gas shells.

On the 8th some student organizations such as Gujarat Students' Circle, Gujarat Students' Federation, Nav Javan Sangh, etc. took out a procession of students against rising prices. Their plan was to set on fire an effigy representing the price rise. However, the leaders of the procession were arrested before they could carry out the programme. Some other student leaders were also arrested on the eve of their meeting at Sardarbag. Except for the destruction of a milk booth and some sporadic stone-throwing incidents, Ahmedabad had a peaceful day.

In Saurashtra, Wankaner observed a bandh in protest against police atrocities in Jetpur. The call was given by the Jana Sangh. Some stone-throwing incidents took place. Police used tear-gas and lathi; 10 policemen and 15 other persons were injured. Savali, a small taluka town in Baroda district, also observed a bandh. There the call was given by the Congress (O).

On the 9th morning, students assembled in the University Senate Hall. There they pledged that they would sacrifice studies to procure essential commodities for the people. For the first time, they openly linked students' problems with those of the masses. And after a few hours the general meeting of the Gujarat University Area Teachers Association (GUATA) took place in the same University Senate Hall. The teachers decided to launch an agitation against the Vice-Chancellor for his pro-management policy. The secretary of GUATA opposed police atrocities in curbing the student agitation.

On the 9th, the students observed a "Vidyarthi Curfew" for three hours from 9 a.m. to 12 noon. Accordingly, students did not allow vehicles, whether private or public, to ply on the roads. Some students lay down on the roads to prevent the movement of vehicles. Some student leaders were arrested. To demand the release of the arrested students, a large procession of students went to the police station. Several stone throwing incidents took place in the city. Foodgrains shops in Dariapur and Lunsawad areas were looted. Seven milk booths were set ablaze. Besides tear-gas shells and lathi charges, police opened fire on the crowd. Several persons were injured in the confrontation. Night curfew was imposed in some parts of the city.

On the same day, the Jana Sangh and the Congress (O) organized a bandh in several towns: Ankleswar, Dharampur, Vicchia, Mahuva, Bagsara, and Vagodia. In Himatnagar of Sabarkantha district, students went on strike to express solidarity with Ahmedabad students. They organized a procession and threw stones at shops and the police. The police lathi-charged the crowd.

On the 14th August, Shramjivi Samiti, dominated by leftists and an organization of several trade unions of white-collar employees including the Jana Sangh and the Congress (O) sympathisers, gave a call for Ahmedabad bandh on January 10 against price-rise and scarcity. It declared that price-rise and scarcity were man-made, and that the Gujarat government had failed to jail the people who were really responsible for the price-rise and scarcity. It was this failure, according to the Samiti, that had led to food riots in Gujarat. The Samiti added that instead of providing essential commodities to the people, the government had used force to curb the demands of the masses. The bandh call of the Samiti was supported by 80 trade unions of the city (mainly of the white-collar employees), various political parties including the Jana Sangh, School Teachers Association, Gujarat University Area Teachers Association, Yuvak Lagni Samiti and various other student organizations. Purshottam Mavalankar, an independent MP, also supported the bandh. And three senior ministers of Chiman Patel's cabinet hailed the students' struggle against the price-rise. They appealed to the students to leave their classes and lead the people.

The city observed almost a total bandh on the 10th. Newspaper offices also did not work. However, the textile mills kept working as the Majoor Mahajan did not support the bandh. From the morning crowds gathered at various places and sporadic stone-throwing incidents started. As the day passed, tension mounted and looting of provision and oil shops began; 30 shops were looted and 20 shops and milk booths were set ablaze. The police fired 57 rounds at 20 places; 52 tear-gas shells were burst at 16 places. Yet the confrontation between the police and the crowd continued throughout the day. And, in spite of the imposition of curfew the riots continued for the next two days. The situation was brought under control on the 13th.

The students of the Baroda University walked out of the classes on the 10th. They threw stones and damaged college and private buildings. While stone-throwing continued, Jana Sangh workers organized a procession, a mile-and-a-half away from the college. It was followed by stone-throwing incidents. During the afternoon two foodgrains shops in Raopura were looted. Riots then spread to several other parts of the city. Foodgrains, oil and kerosene shops were looted. Bus stands and milk booths were set on fire. The police opened fire, burst tear-gas shells and lathi-charged violent crowds. The confrontation between the police and the crowd continued for two days despite the "shoot-at-sight" order. The mood of defiance had caught on.

The battle between the State Reserve Police (SRP) and the people continued in the *poles* (intertwining narrow streets with lanes within lanes) of Ahmedabad on January 10 and 11 and thereafter for two months. The residents of the poles retaliated against police violence in groups. From balconies and terraces, they threw stones at the police. A strong "we" feeling grew among the members of poles and united the residents against the police. The residents of the poles act together to defend any person in the pole. Each pole has its own organization which undertakes social and medical services for the inhabitants. Moreover, the physical structure of the pole is defence-oriented. There is only one entrance. And the main street of the pole is divided into small lanes, each of which is further subdivided until all that remains is just a narrow passage to walk through.[3] Both social homogeneity and physical structure oriented to defence helped the residents in putting up a stubborn fight to the police.

The situation was aggravated by the indiscriminate use of police force in the middle class areas of Ahmedabad. It was reported in the newspapers that the police mercilessly beat up 90-year old persons, a three-year old child, pregnant women etc. Consequently several neutral groups such as pleaders, teachers, Sarvodaya workers, etc. joined the agitation. They condemned police atrocities.

The riots soon spread to other parts of Gujarat. Modasa, Palanpur, Visnagar, and Mehsana in north Gujrat, Bhavnagar and Savarkundala in Saurashtra and Dohad, Jhalod and Khambhat in central Gujarat were engulfed in violence on the 11th and the 12th. Some other cities and towns such as Surat, Bharuch, Prantij, Palitana, Shihore, Salaya, etc. observed bandh on the 10th or the 11th in response to the call of either the Jana Sangh or the Congress (O). On the 12th, more than 16 towns of Gujarat observed bandh. By January 12, most of the urban areas of the state were affected by the food riots of Ahmedabad and Baroda. Thus, the anti-government agitation of the students, political parties and pole organizations of the urban middle class continued simultaneously, and it was difficult to say who led whom. The common feature was the deep-rooted discontent of the masses against the government. It may, however, be added that the anti-government agitation of the peasants came to a halt when urban students and the middle class revolted against the price-rise.

NEW TURN : CHIMAN HATAO

The agitation of the students took a new turn after January 10, in which the masses took an active part. And from education and mess bill problems, the agitation turned to political problems, demanding the resignation of Chiman Patel. The problem of political corruption was taken up and became a major issue in the agitation.

Purshottam Mavalankar was elected from Ahmedabad to the Lok Sabha early in 1973. He was an Independent candidate, supported by the Jana Sangh and the Congress (O), against the ruling Congress. Mavalankar, a professor of political science, was principal of a college. He had many supporters among the students and teachers. After quarrelling with the college management, dominated by the local industrialists, Mavalankar resigned as principal in 1972. He had also certain grievances against Chiman Patel. It should be added that Mavalankar organized a procession of students and teachers in July 1973 in protest against corrupt political practices. At the time when Chiman Patel was trying to become the chief minister by ousting Ghanshyam Oza, Mavalankar submitted a memorandum to the Governor asking him to recommend imposition of President's rule in Gujarat. Mavalankar believed that various political parties looked only after their interests and neglected the problems of the masses. He pleaded that the people should elect only independents who could look after the interests of the people. Some of the leaders of the Yuvak Lagni Samiti were close to Mavalankar. They had worked for him in his election campaign. Mavalankar, through his son who was also a student leader, was closely watching the developments. He supported the Ahmedabad bandh call on the 10th, and came to Ahmedabad from Madras.

Soon after his return he addressed a meeting of students. The next day, i.e. January 11, he again addressed a student meeting. He congratulated the students on launching the agitation. He revived his old demand for the dissolution of the state assembly and imposition of President's rule. He said the government of Gujarat, headed by Chiman Patel, was *bhrashta* (corrupt) and the Congress party had lost the confidence of the people. He appealed to the students and teachers to realize that it was their responsibility to see that honest persons got elected in the elections. Students were responsible not only for expressing the feelings and emotions of the people, but also for the reconstruction of society. Therefore, on Mavalankar's advice and at the suggestion of a journalist, the Yuvak Lagni Samiti was dissolved, and the Navnirman Yuvak Samiti (NYS) war organized in which, besides student representatives of all colleges, some non-student youth were also included; Mavalankar became the President of its advisory committee. However, Mavalankar's association with the Samiti lasted only for four days. On the 15th, he resigned as its president, alleging that before deciding their programmes, the students did not consult him.

On the 14th and 15th, during the Makar Sankrant, a major festival, Gujarat remained more or less calm and people were busy with kite-flying. On the 16th, Jamnagar, Surendranagar, Maliya and Vadhavan in Saurashtra, and Bhuj and Anjar in Kutch, and on the 17th Petlad, Nadiad and other towns of central Gujarat responded to the Jana Sangh call for a bandh. Except for a few stone-throwing incidents, the state remained peaceful. On the 18th, following the Saurashtra bandh call of the Jana Sangh, large scale looting of shops and stone-throwing incidents took place in Rajkot, Junagadh, Gondal and Veraval. Thus, by January 18 more than a hundred cities and towns of Gujarat observed bandh, responding to the Jana Sangh call. The Jana Sangh protested against price-rise but it did not demand Chiman Patel's resignation. It adopted a lukewarm attitude after January 20 towards the agitation of students until the end of the month. Jana Sangh students published handbills criticizing the leaders of the NYS. The party also opposed the call for Gujarat bandh given by the 14th August Shramjivi Samiti and the NYS. And the party alleged that the dissident Congress leaders were responsible for the turmoil in Gujarat.

Meanwhile, the Khedut Samaj, which was leading the anti-levy agitation, became alarmed by the urban riots, which were demanding Chiman Patel's resignation. Though the rich farmers opposed land legislation, they were not against Chiman Patel. They, therefore, went to the rescue of *Khedut putra* (son of a peasant) Chiman Patel. Opposing the demand for the Chief Minister's resignation, Vallabhbhai Patel, a leader of the Khedut Samaj, said the Central government was responsible for corruption and the price rise. The Khedut Samaj withdrew its agitation and declared that farmers would give more paddy in levy than what the government had demanded. In fact, some of its leaders from Saurashtra and south Gujarat moved around villages for collection of the levy.

There was a lull in the situation between January 14 and 16 in Ahmedabad. Many students attended schools and colleges on the 16th. The leaders of the NYS and teachers feared that the agitation would fizzle out if the students attended classes. In order to revive the agitation, the Samiti gheraoed the Vice-Chancellor, Iswarbhai Patel, and also set on fire the furniture and the records of the University. The Samiti demanded closure of the University and colleges till the resignation of the government. The police arrested the President and the Secretary of the Samiti. Stone-throwing incidents followed in the city. The GUATA supported the student agitation against price-rise and condemned police atrocities. It also expressed its willingness to join the agitation against hoarders and corrupt politicians.

On the following day, the Chief Minister called a joint meeting of the Vice-Chancellor, college principals and general secretaries of college unions. The government put forward a proposal for the formation of a committee of general secretaries of the students' union which would negotiate with the government on ways to solve the problems of the students. On the acceptance of the proposal, the government agreed to release the President and Secretary of the NYS. The student leaders agreed to attend schools and colleges from the 19th.

The students, however, rejected the agreement the next day. They said the agreement was imposed on them by the government. The Secretary of the Samiti tore off the agreement papers. The leaders announced that there was no question of attending schools and colleges and that the agitation would continue till the resignation of the government. Two leaders of the Samiti and some teachers were arrested by the police under the MISA. Other important student leaders went underground. Further, the Chief Minister and some of his colleagues tried, without much success, to win over some student leaders of Ahmedabad and elsewhere. The government also accepted all the pending demands of the college teachers. But the teachers and students did not swallow the government bait. They declared that they were fighting for the masses and not for themselves.

The agitation was intensified after the police beating of the girls of the H.K. College on the 21st. School and college girls came out in different cities and towns against the police action. School and college teachers became more active. Leading college professors resigned from the Congress. The GUATA demanded the resignation of the government and of the MLAs and the release of arrested leaders. Several teachers said they would make Chiman Patel a teacher again. Some teachers angrily vowed that they would not allow him even to become a teacher because he would corrupt education. Such was the hatred among teachers against Chiman Patel. The teachers' association provided an important organizational support for spreading the agitation as it had branches in most of the towns in Gujarat. Banners of student-teacher unity went up in many places. The GUATA organized fasts, processions, demonstrations, etc. to mobilize the masses against the Chiman Patel government. It also supported a Gujarat bandh call on January 25, given by the 14th August Shramjivi Samiti and the NYS. It may be added that the business community opposed the call for bandh. The business organizations asked the traders to keep their shops open. The Majoor Mahajan also opposed the bandh. However, the government imposed curfew for 24 to 36 hours in as many as 44 towns of Gujarat. That did not calm the agitation. On the contrary, riots became more widespread.

During this period, some incidents were reported of pole-dwellers of Ahmedabad forcing shop-keepers to open shops and sell commodities at the price declared in *Tankha*, a leaflet published by the NYS and the 14th August Shramjivi Samiti. The business community was alarmed by the incidents. A leading industrialist, Amaritlal Sheth, appealed to the government to provide protection to the traders. It was reported that Chief Minister Chiman Patel assured Sheth that the government would do so. The army was called out in Ahmedabad on January 28. The city remained peaceful for three days. Then began another round of processions, defiance of prohibitory orders, large-scale fasting, stone-throwing, looting and burning of public and private property.

By the end of January, besides teachers, writers, poets, doctors, lawyers and Sarvodaya workers, women's organizations also joined the agitation. Each came forward with one programme or the other to keep the agitation going. Members of the middle class supported the action of the students and others. They thanked the students for voicing their grievances. They did not object to the participation of their children in the agitation. Several parents prompted their sons and daughters to join fasts or processions. In fact, thousands of them, even during the curfew and despite considerable intimidation and often severe repression by the police, participated in the funeral of "martyrs" who had died in police firings. Hundreds of citizens—mostly young people—queued up before hospitals to donate blood for the injured boys. In Baroda and Ahmedabad, more than 200 middle aged women of middle class families took out a procession to police stations where, whole demanding the release of the arrested boys of their localities, they taunted the police in high pitched voice : "You can kill our boys in as large a number as you want. Each of us will produce a hundred sons in their place." The mood of defiance was very intense and widespread, and generally the people's morale was maintained for some time at a high level.

By the first week of February, the agitation had acquired a popular base and could not be ignored by anyone. Hatred for Chiman Patel, who had become the symbol of an anti-people government and of corruption, was widely shared. The President of the state Congress and the dissident leaders had already come out against the chief minister. Then followed the dramatic resignation of a few ministers, and on the advice of the Centre, Chiman Patel himself resigned as chief minister on February 9. The Governor suspended the state assembly and President's rule was imposed on the same day.

DEMAND FOR DISSOLUTION OF ASSEMBLY

The news of Chiman Patel's resignation set off a wave of jubilation in all cities of the state. While the student leaders and teachers were busy celebrating the victory and trying to restore normalcy, the opposition political parties—the Congress (O) and Jana Sangh—declared that the dissolution of the Assembly was the ultimate goal of the agitation. The Secretary of the GPCC (O) declared that the suspension of the Assembly was a "fraud" on the Constitution and was an attempt to deprive the people of their right to elect new representatives. On February 10 the Executive Committee of the GPCC (O) demanded a fresh poll in the state. It declared that people of Gujarat should observe "Dissolution Day" on February 17. Sarvodaya leaders, Ravishankar Maharaj and Jayaprakash Narayan, lent support to the demand. Maharaj appealed to all MLAs to resign from the Assembly to force its dissolution. In the new elections, he said, he would see that no corrupt person was elected.

The leftist parties, the CPI and the CPM, though they demanded the dissolution of the Assembly, wanted effective steps to curb price-rise and also an inquiry into corruption charges. The dissident Congress leaders and the

GPCC chief appealed to all sections of society to restore normalcy.

After a brief period of normalcy, the demand for the dissolution of the Assembly received added momentum with the *en bloc* resignation of 15 Congress (O) MLAs from the State Assembly on February 16. Later, the Congress (O) municipal corporation members of Ahmedabad, Surat and Baroda also resigned to support the demand. The Jana Sangh MLAs and corporators followed suit.

The NYS demanded the dissolution of the state Assembly within "ten days". It launched a fresh agitation. The Samiti prepared a charter of demands which included a judicial inquiry into police firings in the state during the disturbances, withdrawal of the cases against the agitators and "universalisation' of higher education. It should be noted that the charter did not include any economic demands in support of which the Samiti had initially launched the agitation. The teachers, though they rejoined the colleges, supported the demand for the dissolution of the Assembly.

The agitation, which was so far confined to urban areas, spread to the countryside soon after Chiman Patel's resignation. The farmers of Saurashtra, central Gujarat and south Gujarat supported the demand for the dissolution of the Assembly. Bardoli, Navsari, Morvi, Anand, etc. were in the forefront of the agitation. The Gujarat University Syndicate, which was known for its pro-Chiman Patel stand, declared an indefinite closure of the University and demanded dissolution of the Assembly. College principals in Saurashtra region also jumped into the fray.

Businessmen and factory owners also supported the agitation. They observed a bandh to support their demand. In consultation with the mill-owners, the Majoor Mahajan asked workers to abstain from work on March 7 in support of the demand for dissolution of the State Assembly. It is needless to add here that the Majoor Mahajan had opposed the call for Gujarat bandh on January 25, observed in protest against price-rise.

Barring this, the factory workers of Gujarat, as a class, remained indifferent to the agitation both before and after Chiman Patel's resignation. Similarly, the backward classes, except for the students, did not support the agitation. In fact, in Ahmedabad sharp clashes took place between them and the students. In some rural areas it took the form of conflicts between the landed peasantry and the landless who supported the MLAs belonging to the Congress. The urban factory workers and landless labourers felt that the agitation was really not for curbing the price-rise but was politically motivated and directed against the Congress which was sympathetic to the poor.

However, teachers, pleaders, doctors, Sarvodaya workers and other sections of the middle class continued their support to the agitation. Several pole organizations came into existence. They intensified the agitation. At a later stage lawyers boycotted the courts. White-collar employees of banks and the LIC also joined the upsurge; 3.5 lakh employees of the state, central and panchayat administrations went on a day's casual leave to press for the dissolution of the Assembly. The student and non-student youth directed their efforts at persuading the MLAs to resign. By the second week of March, 95 MLAs had resigned from the Assembly. On March 3, more than 500 students from various parts of the state went to Delhi. There they gheraoed the Congress MPs, met Union ministers, organized a procession and demonstrations and launched fasts.

Chiman Patel and his supporters also demanded the dissolution of the state Assembly. And Morarji Desai, the leader of Congress (O), went on an indefinite fast on March 12 in support of this demand.

In the meantime, the riots continued in many cities and towns. Attempts were made to loot banks and co-operative societies. Stone-throwing incidents and looting and burning of public and private property continued on a large scale. Attempts were made to close the borders of the state, so that products of the state did not go out. Violence became widespread. Terror prevailed in the state and nobody could oppose the agitators.

At last, on March 16, the State Assembly was dissolved. All-India Radio, in its last news bulletin, announced the Governor's decision. Thousands of people came out on the streets— even in those areas under curfew. The night turned into a festival. The joyous crowd threw stones at the police and also damaged public property. All political parties, Sarvodaya workers, voluntary associations and students appealed to the people to restore normalcy. Later, schools and colleges reopened and students got busy with their examinations.

2. ORGANIZATION AND LEADERSHIP

As has been seen, the agitation in Ahmedabad had begun with the formation of the Yuvak Lagni Samiti, which was later transformed into the Navnirman Yuvak Samiti (NYS). In Baroda, the Students Action Committee ; in Surat, the Yuvak Sangram Samiti ; in Rajkot and Bhavnagar the Navnirman Samitis came into existence. In other cities, towns, and villages Navnirman Samitis or Sangram Samitis were set up. As the agitation gained momentum, particularly after Chiman Patel's resignation, such samitis were set up at pole and even sub-pole levels by local school and college students and youth, in the beginning at the instance of political leaders. In Ahmedabad city alone more than two hundred such samitis came into existence during February and March. Further, in some cities there were rival organizations of students. For instance, in Rajkot there were two Navnirman Samitis ; in Baroda, a Yuvak Sangram Samiti, and in Surat, a Navnirman Samiti were also organized. Several other organizations such as the Gujarat Students Circle in Ahmedabad, Study and Struggle Alliance in Baroda, Akhil Bharatiya Vidyarthi Parishad, and Tarun Shanti Sena of Sarvodaya Mandal also took an active part in the agitation. Each samiti and organization was independent of the city-level Navnirman Yuvak Samiti or Yuvak Sangram Samiti, and there was no co-ordination among them. Each samiti or organization used to announce various programmes which kept up the tempo of the agitation. We shall deal here, only with the major city-level samitis of Ahmedabad, Baroda, Surat and Rajkot.

The leaders of the main city-level samitis largely came from the upper middle income group. They were the sons of white-collar employees (particularly managers and officials), businessmen or industrialists and belonged to upper castes. In the taluka towns such as Morvi, Padra, Bardoli, Anand, etc. the student leadership was dominated by the sons of the rich farmers and Patidar by caste. Most of the office-bearers of these organizations were elected representatives of college or university unions.

The student leaders can be divided into two categories : the radicals and the rebels. The former were consciously pro-poor and against injustice in society. The latter enjoyed any act of defiance of authority regardless of whether it helped or harmed the rich, poor or anyone, including students themselves. They used words and phrases borrowed from others without understanding their meaning. They were weak in argument and lacked confidence in across-the-table discussions. Therefore, they were prone to lose their temper quickly and took to direct action.

Like the politicians against whom they revolted, they gave promises which could never be fulfilled. They were damago-gues. They often emphasized not only traditional symbols but also traditional values. For instance, a member of the NYS said at a public meeting of two thousand students in Bardoli :

Indira is not Mataji (mother). She is worse than a witch. In olden days people did not allow even the shadow of a widow to fall on them as this was considered inaus-picious. There must be some meaning in that belief. Today, because of this widow there is corruption and rising prices (applause).

Such leaders had many fans and followers. Their example was followed by many students. And their importance was boosted by newspapers and politicians.

The radical student leaders, on the other hand, were few in number and did not have many fans and followers. But they were respected by the general student community and others. They had to depend on popular, rebellious leaders for collecting large crowds and for carrying out the programmes. The rebellious leaders also depended on the radicals during negotiations with university authorities and government officials. They drafted memoranda, appeals and press notes. In general, the radical student leaders were against business-men and industrialists, and they emphasized the need for social change and for eradication of poverty. Manishi Jani, President of the NYS, focussed on poverty in his verses and speeches. He believed in a classless society which would be brought about with a more equitable distribution of wealth and a better deal for the working class.[4] Another student leader, Bhagirath Shah of the Yuvak Sangram Samiti, Surat, also believed in a classless society. He said that the dissolution of the Assembly marked only an "initial victory" for the student movement against "rising prices and corruption". According to him, for "final victory" student must seek an "alliance with the industrial working class and the rural poor."[5].

Some student leaders had been attracted by Indira Gandhi's call for Garibi Hatao, and were once close to the Ruling Congress. Because of their faith in pro-poor policies of Indira Gandhi, as opposed to the policies of the Jana Sangh and the Congress (O), these leaders made all attempts during the agitation to counter the "Indira Hatao" call given by the opposition parties and the farmers lobby. They also did not respond to parochial demands like redressal of alleged injustice done to Gujarat. Barring a few, the radical student leaders did not, however, have any concrete programme to direct the agitation. They wanted to eradicate poverty and control price-rise, but they did not know how to do it. They talked about "reconstruction" of the society, but they could not spell out their vision of the new society for which they were fighting. Kanu Bhavsar, a member of the NYS, said, "we wanted to touch the basic issues of society like poverty and inequality but we do not know what to do for that. We are in confusion and darkness"[6]. Many others shared Bhavsar's perplexity.

There was no inhibition as regards violence. In fact, the radical as well as the rebellious leaders advocated violence in public. They believed that non-violence was out of date. "Even Gandhi would not have advised non-violence in the present conditions", a member of the Surat Yuvak Sangram Samiti said at a public meeting. During the early period of the agitation, another member of the NYS asked the students to take to "guerilla warfare". One of the top-ranking leaders of the NYS said at a public meeting at Bardoli :

We do not believe in non-violence or violence, but we should reply to the police in its own language. Our students are revolutionaries, stone in one hand, and iron manhole covers in the other... Gandhi was talking about non-violence because he was wearing a "langoti" while we have terylene clothes, and therefore we cannot follow Gandhi's advice... There are many government buildings which are still untouched by us. We want to bring them down...

Apparently, the student leaders were not members of any political party. In Ahmedabad, the main leaders of the NYS were not members of any political party, and they made this quite clear from the beginning. They abused not only the Congress but also other political parties, from the Jana Sangh to the Communists. But many of the leaders had personal loyalty to one political leader or another. In Baroda, Surat, and Rajkot, the student leaders had close links with the Jana Sangh, Congress (O), or one of the factions of the Congress party. Student leaders got help in cash or kind—vehicles, telephones, hotel accomodation etc.—from rich political leaders. They also sought advice and guidance from the latter.

The Executive Committee of the NYS, Ahmedabad, and other city level samitis in other cities hardly met during the agitation. The main seven or eight leaders used to meet informally at someone's place, an hour after the scheduled time. They hardly transacted any serious business. They would gossip about several things, from sex to politics. Meanwhile, someone would suggest some programme for the next day which others accepted with little or no discussion. Someone, mostly a non-student, a teacher, a journalist, or a political leader would prepare a press note about the programme. More often than not, other members of the samitis came to know of the programmes only through press notes. Sometimes, different student leaders amnounced different programmes and the press found it difficult to know which programmes were genuine.

Needless to say, the programmes were not planned in any detail. The student leaders were not sure why they preferred a particular programme to others. Most programmes had only a symbolic value. Whenever any serious programme, which involved planning and time, such as picketing or distribution of handbills or undertaking signature campaigns, etc., was suggested, the leaders showed little interest in it. It would appear that they were interested in press notes or in seeing their names and photographs in print. If, for some reason, a newspaper failed to publish their press notes with their names, the leaders were annoyed and quarrelled with the reporters. Before their release from jail, these leaders often called photographers and their friends to receive them. Sometimes, in order to help others organise receptions, they would stay longer in jail or spend a few hours outside the city.

During the early phase of the agitation, the student leaders were relatively united. In Ahmedabad, some leaders were in jail and others went underground; so they did not meet each other. But slowly their unity declined and differences developed among them. Often they quarrelled over petty issues, largely the result of misunderstanding or temperamental behaviour. Besides, in Rajkot, Surat, and Baroda, the rivalry between the Congress (O) and Jana Sangh student leaders intensified. At the same time, they got united against radical students. After the Gujarat bandh on January 25, radical students who were a few in number were isolated and were also beaten up by the Jana Sangh sympathisers.

Serious differences among the leaders of the NYS came to surface in the last phase of the agitation. A section of the Samiti accepted the invitation of Gokhale, the Union Law Minister, to visit New Delhi. But some others, mainly supporters of the Jana Sangh, the Congress (O) and Chiman Patel (who, ironically, had after his expulsion from the Congress, thrown his support behind the agitation) opposed the Samiti's move. They were interested in continuing the agitation. They therefore, tried to prevent the students from going to New Delhi and, after they had managed to go, denounced them openly.

Besides youth and student samitis and organizations, school and college teachers' association, Bar associations, Sarvodaya mandals, mahila parishads, journalists' associations, etc., different political parties also actively participated in the agitations. They announced their own programmes and tried to boost the morale of the students. Particularly, some teachers and journalists worked as friends, guides and philosophers to the students at many places. For instance, when the student leaders of the NYS were either in jail or underground, they used to issue press notes and appeals in the name of some student leaders and encouraged the second rank leadership of the NYS to sustain the tempo of the agitation. Ravishankar Maharaj and Jayaprakash Narayan, the Sarvodya leaders, also raised the students' morale by their open support.

3. ISSUES AND PROGRAMMES

The agitation was not carried out by a single organization or political party. Several hundred groups participated in it. Therefore, it had diffused objectives varying from group to group. As has been observed, the agitation began with the protest against price rise and scarcity of foodgrains. Slowly, as the agitation continued, other issues such as resignation of Chiman Patel, dissolution of the state Assembly, misuse of MISA, police atrocities, injustice to Gujarat and Gujaratis, construction of Narmada dam, etc., entered the picture. Certain issues got currency and others did not.

The radical student leaders and teachers of Ahmedabad who had started the agitation wanted to use the agitation to highlight the economic hardships of masses. They were against hoarders, blackmarketeers and capitalists. They therefore, supported the 14th August Shramjivi Samiti. In the handbill, *Tankha* (spark), jointly issued by the 14th August Shramjivi and the Navnirman Yuvak Samiti, they declared :

> People want cheap and good quality foodgrains. People do not want the charity of the shethiyas (capitalists); people also do not want dramatic announcements by the ministers; nor do they want a farce in the name of levy... Price rise can only be fought by strong implementation of the levy, by nationalizing the business of edible oil, by jailing black-marketeers and hoarders.

They demanded eight kgs of good quality foodgrains per individual. They appealed to people to form Roji Roti Samitis in every pole, which should start picketing shops and keeping a watch on prices and quality of articles. They also appealed for the formation of an alliance of students and workers.

For some time, in Ahmedabad, Bhavnagar and many other cities, the traders were forced to sell certain commodities at fixed reduced prices. In Surat, radical student leaders made

organized attempts to maintain the price line of certain commodities and control distribution. The Yuvak Sangram Samiti
formed a corps of volunteers to supervise the maintenance of
price line, prevent adulteration and other malpractices of the
traders. With the help of the Collector and District Supply
Officer (DSO), the supply of vegetable oil and sugar was entrusted to co-operative societies and fair price shops instead of the
traders. A fixed quota of both commodities at a reduced price
was supplied to all families of the city on ration cards. They
also identified hoarders and wholesalers and forced the police
and DSO to raid their godowns. A women's organization of
Surat, Stri Shakti, mainly composed of students, mobilized
slum dwellers and organized processions demanding construction of latrines, drainage and provision of water facilities instead
of the construction of a town-hall. It denounced bureaucratiza-
tion. In Baroda, the Study and Struggle Alliance, a student organization, moved around the working class areas and tried to
establish links with them. The Alliance formed mohalla (area)
committees and also organized processions demanding a ration
quota of 12 kg. of foodgrains per individual per month. In Vedchhi, Adivasi college students went to villages, gheraoed landlords
and forced them to pay at least Rs. 3 per day to the agricultural
labourers. However, no permanent organization or machinery
was set up by the radical students to lessen the economic hardships of the masses. Barring these few isolated instances where
the local radical students sought the help of the people, the
NYS did nothing significant to fulfil its economic demands. It
did not even organize symbolic programmes to highlight the
economic issues. No Roji Roti Samiti was set up either in
Ahmedabad or elsewhere. The call for an alliance of students
and workers went unheeded. In fact, the working class
conspicuously remained out of the agitation. The NYS did
not have any machinery even to distribute handbills.

Except for expressing support for the agitation through press
notes, the leftist parties, the CPI and the CPM, played almost
no part in the agitation. They did not organize public meetings or processions. They were virtually onlookers. At the
most they used to discuss 'kranti', i.e. revolution, in the abstract
for several hours a day. Or, they branded the agitation as
'counter-revolution'. The Sarvodaya workers were concerned

with such issues as violence and non-violence, corruption, etc. They organized processions and satyagrahas for establishing peace. But they were more concerned with ousting Chiman Patel and bringing about the dissolution of the Assembly than educating the people about economic problems.

The radical teachers of Ahmedabad, no doubt, considered economic problems important, but they were obsessed with removing Chiman Patel from power. They therefore, highlighted corruption and put forward programmes which were taken up by [rebellious student leaders, Congress (O), Jana Sangh, Vidyarathi Parishad, and middle class pole-dwellers. During the latter part of the agitation, these organizations, political parties and pole samitis imposed several stunt programmes on the NYS.

Besides strikes and bandhs, several processions were organized in all cities and towns by the Navnirman or Sangram Samitis, mainly demanding Chiman Patel's resignation and the dissolution of the State Assembly. These included silent processions ; processions with empty tins of oil and empty bags symbolizing the scarcity of essential commodities ; procession depicting Congress leaders and MLAs as animals or stones ; and mock funeral of Chiman Patel and other Congress leaders (at places, also of Indira Gandhi). Sometimes as many as a hundred effigies were burnt in a day in Ahmedabad. Children and young school boys were very active in these programmes which sometimes led to stone-throwing incidents and rioting.

The medical students of Ahmedabad, Baroda and Surat performed mock surgery on Chiman Patel and other Congress leaders. They declared that they found edible oil, grains, currency notes, etc. from the body of the operated leaders. Girl students of Ahmedabad held a mock court. The "Court" charged Chiman Patel and others with acts of corruption and mismanagement.

Gheraoes and dharnas directed at the Congress leaders and MLAs were common. Demonstrators demanded their resignation from the Assembly, the municipal Corporation and the party. The houses of the leaders were stoned. They were presented with bangles, sarees and brassiers, implying that they were effeminate, incapable of raising their voice in support of the masses.   They were also given bread prepared from bajra sold at ration shops to show them what kind of food people were being forced to eat.   Bottles of blood, to show that the students were ready to shed the last drop of their blood if the government wanted it as price for its resignation, were handed over to the Congress leaders.   Vehicles of the Gongressmen were damaged or burnt.   Their houses were set on fire.   Water, electricity and telephone connections were cut.   Some Congress leaders were beaten up and insulted by the mobs.   One Congress leader was not only stripped naked, but was forced to walk several miles from village to village.   Student mobs painted the face of an MLA black and forced him to ride a donkey.   The Speaker of the State Assembly was beaten up in a hospital.   Slogan-shouting and loud demonstrations lasting several hours took place every day in front of the residence of Congressmen.   At an appointed time in the evening the now well-known "thali-beating" demonstrations took place in the major towns—signifying the death-knell of the Chiman Patel government.   State transport buses and trucks were hijacked. In Ahmedabad as many as 37 buses were hijacked by the students in a single day.   Similar incidents took place in other places and taluka towns.   Various forms of fasts in public places opposite government offices, houses of MLAs, Corporators' offices and almost in every pole were observed.   Signature campaigns demanding dissolution of the Assembly were undertaken.   Public opinion polls for MLA's resignations and dissolution of the Assembly were conducted in some towns.

Most significantly, radical students, teachers, political parties, including the Jana Sangh, Congress (O) and Communists, Sarvodaya Mandals and some other voluntary organizations made all efforts to see that the agitation did not turn into communal riots.   Whenever a communal colour was sought to be given to the agitation, it was condemned.   And, in order to avoid clashes between Hindus and Muslims, the NYS and other organizations did not put forward any programme on the day of Moharrum and Holi. They repeatedly appealed to the people to maintain communal harmony.   Collective prayers of Hindus and Muslims were also held in which the leaders of the NYS recited Quran and Gita.

4. CONCLUSION

Spiralling prices and scarcity of essential commodities and inadequacy of basic amenities in urban areas provided the breeding ground for the unprecedented upsurge in Gujarat. Discontent against the government was deep and widespread. People in general, and the middle class in particular, had increasingly felt that they were powerless and were being alienated from the political system. Their fury was against excessive manipulation and corruption in politics, in which the common man had no voice. Acceptance of direct action and violence to solve problems had become widespread among all sections of society. Tension gradually mounted and soon turned into rioting and violence.

It was essentially an urban middle class agitation. Being unorganized and diffused in its interests, the middle class could not direct the agitation. It supported and participated in all anti-government protests, whether it helped or harmed the middle class itself. On the one hand, it followed the organized interest groups and political parties, and, on the other, it also sometimes initiated *ad hoc* and impulsive programmes to ventilate their grievances against hawkers, milkmen, bus drivers, bus conductors, traders, industrialists and politicians. The programmes were locality-based and unorganized. However, they kept up the tempo of the agitation. When Khadiya was calm, disturbances started in Maninagar. Similarly, when Ahmedabad was about to return to normalcy, riots started in Baroda, then in Rajkot and so forth. This is the strength and weakness of the agitation led by unorganized groups.

Students, one of the more organized sections of the middle class, spearheaded the agitation. Most of the students who participated in the agitation were rebellious, and enjoyed the thrill of revolt and defiance of authority. During the agitation, they felt a sense of power and self-importance. But they lacked direction, commitment and sense of purpose. Significantly, except perhaps in dress-style and relations with the opposite sex, their values did not differ much from those of their parents and the ruling class. Needless to say, there were a few radical students who were the brain behind the agitation. In the course of the agitation, they were, however, isolated by the political parties and the rebellious students. Though they had a sense of purpose and direction, they lacked organization and cadre. And they were also confused about their immediate and future programmes. Under the direction of the radical leaders, the Navnirman and other Samitis tried in the beginning to link up their problems with those of the larger society. But because of their *ad hoc* approach, lack of organization and direction they merely became instruments of organized groups; they lost track of their own objectives. The student agitation in Gujarat suggests that students can overthrow a government and yet be unable to become an independent force for political change.

College teachers in Gujarat, who were well organized through their associations, had deep-rooted grievances against Chiman Patel. They were determined to oust him as soon as he came to power. They, along with certain intellectuals and political leaders of the opposition parties, directed the students' revolt against the Chief Minister. In doing so, despite the fact that some of the leaders of teachers' association were radicals, they undermined the economic programmes of the NYS. They were hardly able to rise above their trade union (GUATA) activities. Later on, after Chiman Patel's resignation, the Congress (O), Jana Singh, Sarvodaya Mandal, businessmen, and rich peasants undermined the economic programmes of the agitation such as lowering of prices, and directed the agitation to political ends—mainly the dissolution of the State Assembly. The radical students and teachers were helpess against the powerful and organized forces on the one hand, and the unorganized rebellious students, on the other. The latter were led by the organized political parties and interest groups.

The faction-ridden Congress party also did not stand united against the agitation. Some Congress leaders worked as catalysts in intensifying the agitation. The ordinary members of the party were confused.

The middle class agitation in Gujarat began on the issues of price rise and scarcity, but succeeded under the shrewd guidance of organized interest groups and parties in ousting Chiman Patel and dissolving the State Assembly. As the dust began to settle down, people were feeling that the basic issues

for which they had revolted for two months had remained
unsolved.   In fact, the price rise and scarcity had worsened.

NOTES

1. Ghanshyam Shah, "Anatomy of Urban Riots : Ahmedabad 1973"
    Economic and Political Weekly, Vol. IX, Nos. 6,7 and 8, Annual
    Number, February 1974.
2. *Gujarat Samachar*, December 23, 1973.
3. H. L. Doshi, *"Traditional Neighbourhood in a Modern City"*, Delhi,
    Abhinav Publishers, 1974.
4. *Times Weekly*, Vol. 4, No. 34, March 24, 1974.
5. *The Free Press Bulletin*, April 16, 1974.
6. Interview.

BIHAR

Introduction

The 1950s were considered India's 'most dangerous decade'.[1] The danger was seen to stem from centrifugal and parochial forces. The country's competitive political system and mixed economy succeeded to some extent in containing the communal, caste and regional forces. A degree of national integration and unity was attained. But again a crisis arose in the late sixties and the early seventies, and this time it proved to be of a more serious nature. It is at once a political and an economic crisis. If it is not resolved, not only will economic and social discontent mount even national unity and integration will be seriously affected and turn out to be 'phoney'.[2]

For the first time since independence, basic assumptions of parliamentary democracy came to be questioned after 1972 by intellectuals and politicians. Doubts were also raised about the capacity of the present political system to solve the country's socio-economic problems. The legitimacy of the electoral system itself as also the representative character of the elected legislators and the political parties had been widely questioned. Direct action for pressurising and overthrowing the government was being widely justified. The Bihar movement of 1974-75 only exemplified the situation.

The Bihar movement under the leadership of Jayaprakash Narayan did not aim at bringing about a few changes here and there. It aimed at 'total revolution' in the country. It challenged the existing political system and sought to change it. It also wanted to bring about changes in economic, educational and other systems. The present study focuses on this 'total revolution' aspect of the movement.

In common paralance, the term revolution is used interchangeably with reform, rebellion and revolt but they need to be distinguished from one another. Reform does not challenge the government or the political system. It attempts to bring about changes in relations between the parts of the system to make it more efficient, responsive and workable A revolt is a challenge to political authority. It is an attempt to overthrow the government, often without prior organization of the masses for the struggle and without any clear set of alternative social and political order. A rebellion is an attack on existing authority without any intention to seize state power. It challenges the prevailing values and institutions in society, but it does not envisage alternative institutions to establish a new social order. A rebellion begins with the feeling that "we can change the way things are," but it usually does not stipulate the direction of such change in any systematic manner, beyond saying "they ought to do this and they ought to do that".[3]

In a revolution, on the other hand, a section or sections of society launch an organized struggle to overthrow not only the established government and regime but also the socio-economic structure which sustains it, and replace the structure with an alternative social o der.[4] Revolutionaries have to evolve an effective organization and cadre, long-term strategies and short-term tactics to make a revolutionary movement a success.[5] Thus the prerequisites of a revolutionary movement are :

(1) An ideology, which presents a profile, general or specific, of the future social order, such as Ram Rajya, socialism, or people's democracy etc. This serves to give a direction to the movement.

(2) Programmes and strategies, which concretize the ideology. Obviously, the programmes must be acceptable to the followers of and particiants in the movement.

(3) Personnel, which comprises leaders, who understand the ideology and cadre, who carry out programmes.

(4) An organization linking the revolutionaries at various levels through communication and action.

The Bihar movement will be examined with reference to these prerequisites.

Since a movements takes place in a given society at a particular point of time, the first chapter examines briefly the salient features of the society and politics of Bihar.

Usually, some incidents take place before the start of a

'movement'. The second chapter deals with the antecedents of the movement.

The third chapter assesses the movement with reference to the prerequisites mentioned above.

The fourth chapter deals with the ideology of the movement, namely the Sarvodaya ideology.

The fifth (and the concluding) chapter is an appraisal of the movement and its future.

The present study is based on the material collected during my three visits to Bihar, the first in August 1974, the second in November 1974, and the third in March-April 1975. In all, I spent about eight weeks in Bihar, visiting some district and block towns and villages. I interviewed activists as well as opponents of the movement. Among the people I interviewed were students, teachers, Sarvodaya workers, leaders of different political parties, businessmen and common people. I have also used newspaper reports. The study is confined to the fiirst year—March 1974 to 1975—of the movement.

NOTES

1. Selig S. Harrison, *India : The Most Dangerous Decade.* Bombay, Oxford University Press, 1960.
2. See, J. D. Sethi. *India In Crisis,* Delhi, Vikas Publishing House Pvt. Ltd., 1975; B. G. Verghese. The Hour of Decision, *Sunday World* March 24 and 31, 1974; Rajni Kothari, Integration and Performance; Two Pivots of India's Model of Nation-building, (mimeographed), Delhi, Centre For the Study of Developing Societies 1975.
3. James and Grace Lee Boggs, *Revolution and Evolution in the Twentieth Century,* New York, Monthly Review Press, 1974.
4. *Ibid.* See also John Dunn, *Modern Revolution, An Introduction to the Aralysis of a Political Phenomenon,* London, Cambridge University Press, 1972.
5. For similar analysis, see I. P. Desai, *The Vedchhi Movement: A History of Rural Development in Modern India,* Vol. II by I.P. Desai and Banwarilal Choudhry. New Delhi Impex India, 1977.

1

Society and Politics in Bihar

Bihar is a landlocked territory in eastern India, surrounded by Nepal in the north, West Bengal in the east, Uttar Pradesh and Madhya Pradesh in the west, and Orrissa in the south. Topographically, the state can be divided into three important parts : North Bihar Plain, South Bihar Plain, and Chhotanagpur Plateau. This is also the rough division in terms of economic activity. The alluvial soil of North Bihar makes the land fertile, but it is flooded annually by the waters of the Ganga and several other rivers, big and small. South Bihar, except for a few isolated hills on the southern and eastern fringe, is also alluvial. The Chhotanagpur Plateau, hilly and covered with forests and one of the richest mineral belts in India, is drought prone, as is the barren hilly area of South Bihar.

Bihar is called 'a rich country inhabited by poor people.'[1] It is rich in minerals, producing 46 per cent of the country's coal, 45 per cent of bauxite, 82 per cent of copper and 88 per cent of kyanite. It has capital-intensive industrial units such as the steel complexes at Bokaro and Jamshedpur, the heavy engineering complex at Ranchi and the refinery at Barauni. And yet, Bihar is one of the poorest states in the country. Its agricultural output per acre is lower than the all-India average. Its per capita income was Rs. 215 in 1968-69 and was estimated at Rs. 225 in 1973-74, the lowest among all the states of the country. The average growth rate of per capita income was a mere 0.26 per cent between 1961-62 and 1968-69. Almost three-fourths of the population live below poverty line, that is, their per capita monthly consumer expenditure is

Rs. 20 or less.

Almost every year hundreds of people die in flood, famine and epidemics. In 1974, for instance, 22,000 people died of smallpox and several hundreds were disabled and disfigured. The rate of infant mortality is one of the highest in the country—nearly 45.11 per thousand among males and 37.52 per thousand among females. Health services in Bihar are inadequate. There is on an average one doctor per 24,000 rural population as against the national norm of one doctor per 17,000 persons. Other basic amenities are also inadequate. For instance, out of 67,645 villages in Bihar, 6,312 do not have drinking water within a radius of one mile.[2]

Hindus, who form more than 80 per cent of Bihar population, can be classified into four categories : upper ('twice-born') castes, middle castes, lower castes, and Harijans or scheduled castes. The other communities are Muslims and scheduled tribes or Adivasis, forming 13.48 and 9.1 per cent respectively of the state population. Adivasis are mainly concentrated in Chhotanagpur. Though Muslims are found all over the state, they are mainly concentrated in Patna, Gaya and Muzaffarpur districts.

The thirty sub-divisions of the lower castes together form the single largest group, nearly 32 per cent of the population. The scheduled castes, even poorer, form 14 per cent of the total population but are scattered all over the state. The upper castes (Brahmin, Bhumihar, Rajput and Kayastha), though forming only 13.6 per cent of the population, occupy a dominant position not only in social but also in economic and political life. The middle castes (Yadav, Kurmi and Koiri), forming 18.7 per cent of the total population of the state,[3] have lately been coming up in politics.

Social and economic inequality is glaring in Bihar. Social mobility is very limited. Political power is concentrated in the hands of the upper caste and class groups.

We shall now analyse the different occupational groups and their role in Bihar politics.

1. THE RURAL SETTING

There is very little diversification of occupational structure in Bihar. Nearly 82 per cent of the working force is engaged in agriculture, 43 percent as cultivators and 39 per cent as agricultural labourers. Most of the landowners are from the Brahmin, Bhumihar and Rajput castes. Only 5.7 per cent of the other castes own land. On the other hand, 92 per cent of the agricultural labourers come from scheduled castes, scheduled tribes, middle and low castes.[1]

Land in Bihar is concentrated in a few hands. 0.4 per cent, having more than 50 acres of land, hold 6.5 per cent of the total agricultural land. Another 5 per cent, owning more than 15 but less than 50 acres of land, hold 26.3 per cent of the total agricultural land. Thus 5.4 per cent of the agricultural families hold 33 per cent of the total agricultural land. Those among them who have adopted modern methods of agriculture using fertilizers, improved seeds, tractors and irrigation facilities, have become richer after independence.

About 23 per cent of farmers have land ranging from 5 to 15 acres.[5] They can be classified into two groups. One group, the numerically larger and mostly found in South Bihar and Chhotanagpur, has not received irrigation and other facilities and has consequently stayed poor. The second group consists of farmers who have got irrigation facilities. They have improved their economic condition during the last two decades, for instance, farmers in Chandi block of Biharsharif where there were 1952 tube wells in 1974, with electric or diesel pumps. In Chandi the use of chemical fertilizers increased almost three-fold between 1971-72 and 1974-75. The production of cash crops like sugarcane and tobacco increased. The farmers demanded more fertilizers, seeds, electricity and higher prices for their produce but resented the government levy. This applied also to some other blocks in Patna, Gaya, Shahabad, Champaran and Monghyr districts. But only 24.8 per cent of the total area sown in Bihar was irrigated in 1970-71. Thus, on the whole, the group of newly rich farmers is relatively small and concentrated in certain districts of the state. These neo-rich with middle-size land holding and rich farmers having more than 15 acres of land form the landed class of Bihar.

On the other hand, 71.6 per cent of the total cultivating households have less than 5 acres of land. One-half of these have less than two and a half acres of land. These are doubtless uneconomic holdings. The small size of land holding and lack of irrigation facilities, on the one hand, and rising prices of fertilizers, seeds and other facilities, on the other, compel small farmers to sell their land. Every year, 4 per cent of the small cultivators sell off their land. According to one estimate, the number of annual sale of agricultural land has increased three fold during the last 25 years.[6] The number of agricultural labourers increased from 23 per cent in 1961 to 39 per cent in 1971. A part of this increase may be attributed to definitional changes in the census categories, but many small cultivators must have turned agricultural labourers to save their land.

Agriculture labourers get their wages in kind or in cash at the rate of Re. 1 or Rs. 1.50 per day. They hardly get work for more than 200 days a year. During the remaining part of the year they are paid even less than this, if they get any work at all. During the slack season, when they are forced to live near the starvation line, the land-holders lend them money at high rates of interest and keep them under their subjugation.[1]

In south Bihar and in some other parts of the state, money-lenders-cum-landlords make the landless labourers work for them permanently. This system is known a 'Saunkia'. In his survey, Father Saupin observes :

In the Saunkia system as practised here, if a man takes a loan of any amount, he will have to work for the money-lender as and when required till the loan is paid back. He gets a morning breakfast, a mid-day meal and two 'kachchi seers' ($2\frac{1}{2}$ lbs.) of paddy, maize or dal. With this 'one seer' he will have to feed his family and pay back the loan. Salt, oil and other things are not considered. To further intimidate these poor people, if they absent themselves from work for any reason, be it sickness, marriage or visiting a relative, they incur a debt of Rs. 2 for every day they are absent. They just cannot fight back and so bow under the inevitable and keep working. The only respite they might get is when there is no work on contract labour, and even then, very often, a portion of their hard-won earnings are taken from them to pay back an ever-increasing loan over which they have no check.[8]

The above description is applicable to practically the whole of Bihar, differing only in degree from region to region. Landless labourers are not yet politically conscious. They blame their fate for this plight. To them the moneylender, the landlord or the government servant is their *malik*, i.e. lord. The communist parties have organized landless labourers at some places, but these organizations are of a local nature.

LAND OWNING AND POLITICAL POWER

The landed class—landlords, rich and neo-rich farmers—enjoys a dominant position in the political and administrative processes of the state. During the freedom movement zamindars were active within the Congress. In the thirties they frustrated the efforts of the socialist and other radicals in the party to give a radical orientation to the economic policy of the Congress. In 1937, the Bihar Provincial Congress Committee went so far as to pass a resolution asking all Congress workers and sympathisers to 'keep themselves aloof' from the activities of the Kisan Sabha, radical peasants' organization.[9] They also opposed some of the radical-sounding measures of Congress from outside. K.N. Singh of Hazaribagh organized the Janta Party in 1949, "to drive out the Congress from Chhotanagpur and Santhal Parganas and cleanse Bihar politics of casteism, corruption and to restore the Zamindari rights."[10] In 1959, the Janata Party merged with the Swatantra Party. However, on account of difference with Swatantra leaders, Singh and his supporters joined the Congress in 1964 but walked out in 1967 because they failed to secure Congress tickets for all their nominees in the fourth general election, and joined the Jana Kranti Dal. Soon after, when the Dal split, some of the members joined the Congress party and some the Jana Sangh. Thus the landed class exercises its influence through the Congress, Congress (O), Jana Sangh and Swatantra Party. After the 1967 Assembly elections when non-Congress parties came to power, more than three-fourths of the total number of M.L.A.s belonged to the landed class.[11]

Outside the party framework, the landed class has district level organizations in some parts of north and south Bihar. They are known as Krishak Sangh or Kisan Sangh. Their aim is to protect and advance the interests of farmers, including the procuring of seeds, fertilizers and irrigation facilities, and arranging for the sale of their crops at 'proper prices'. The Sanghs have the support of the Congress as well as the Jana Sangh.

Like political leaders, 83 per cent of the bureaucrats at different levels in Bihar belong to the upper castes.[12] It may be recalled that in 1954 the secretariat employees came out on the streets to protest against land reform measures.[13] The Central Land Reform Committee noted :

> The lower echelons of the revenue administration found themselves overawed by the big landowners who were not only the leaders of rural society but were also the men who wield considerable authority in the political parties that mattered.[14]

If the local officials were 'overawed' by the landlords, the higher officers in the secretariat had a direct interest in maintaining the *status quo* in the countryside. A Bihar official, for instance, felt that the registering of tenants and giving them (tenants) their due were "bound to upset the social order of things".[15] Obviously, since the officials were not interested in "upsetting the order", they allowed loopholes to remain in land reform legislations. They also sabotaged the Acts at the implementation level. The Bihar Revenue Secretary issued the following instructions to the lower level officials, which put an end to the registration of tenants :

> Reports have been received that in spite of clear instructions some field officers and staff have started recording under-raiyats (tenants). *This should stop at once,* Until further orders no work relating to recording of under-raiyats should be taken up during the Drive (special drive for recording the tenants) period. Even preliminary work relating to collection of data about possession of under-raiyats... should be kept in abeyance... Circle Inspectors and Karmacharis (village accountants) should be specially *warned* to follow these instructions carefully. Persons found violating these instructions will be seriously dealt with. Treat most urgent.[16]

No wonder that the 'progressive' land reform Acts have not been seriously implemented in Bihar. "Happy fraternization between state functionaries and landlords"[17] is a striking spectacle even to a casual observer. In 1971, a 'private army' consisting of armed goondas hired by landlords raided the paddy land of the poor Santhal sharecroppers, set fire to their huts and killed at last ten Santhals. "The police recovered the bodies and seized the tractor some 40 hours after the killings."[13] The political workers who organized poor peasants were harassed, intimidated and in extreme cases, murdered by the landed class with the connivance of government officials and state machinery. The following two incidents from Palamau district, reported by *The Economic and Political Weekly*, are illustrations :

Sachchidanand Prasad, a social worker of Ranka, had taken up cases of evicted tribals in 1969, when the state was under a non-Congress government. All his efforts for almost three years resulted in nothing, he could not get even a hearing from the concerned officials, despite the dozens of petitions he wrote to the authorities, including successive chief ministers of the state and the Prime Minister of the country. On the contrary, the evicted tribals were intimidated and Sachchidanand Prasad himself was beaten up and implicated in a theft and rape case. (He was later acquitted by the court). The other incident involves Theodore Kujur, who was the only person who could read and write in his village, Humia. He used to help the people fight against moneylenders. So he was murdered. There was nothing mysterious about the circumstances of his muder; the only mystery was how the name of the suspect mentioned in the first information was dropped in the charge-sheet submitted by the police (Case No. 189 of 1971).[12]

Thus, whenever poor peasants and labourers got organized and asserted their rights the state machinery was set in motion in protect rich farmers. And, on the pretext of maintaining law and order, the *status quo* in economic and political power structure was maintained.

2.   THE URBAN SETTING

Unrest in urban Bihar was widespread. But the nature of

the unrest was different from that in the countryside. Only about 10 per cent of the population lives in towns. Of these, 41 per cent (belonging mostly to lower castes and usually casual workers) live below the poverty line. They are unorganized and marginalized both socially and politically.

Then, there are industrial workers. In 1970, the total number of factories in Bihar was 16,485 which employed about 2,71,619 workers. Employment in manufacturing industries increased between 1961 and 1971 from 2.2 per cent to 5.1 per cent. The number of workers in mining and household industries, however, declined from 8.9 per cent in 1961 to 2.5 per cent in 1971.

Most factory and mine workers are organized in trade unions, most of them controlled by the Indian National Trade Union Congress (INTUC) and a few by the communist parties and the Socialist Party. Though the economic condition of the workers has not improved much in relation to the actual cost of living, industrial unrest in Bihar has, on the whole, been contained.

The industrial magnates, factory owners and proprietors of commercial firms, largely non-Biharis or Biharis belonging to upper castes, and forming altogether less than 3 per cent of the population, enjoy a dominant position. They are better organized than any other section of society. Through their organizations, press and public relations they have their way with the government both at the policy level and at the implementation level. Like the landed class, they are in the Congress, Congress (O), Jana Sangh and Bharatiya Lok Dal. They are critical of income tax and sales tax, of the licencing policy and other regulatory rules of the government. The president of the Bihar Chamber of Commerce said that 'corruption' and black marketing and other ills of society were due to government's restrictions on trade and industry.[20] At the same time, the Chamber gives sumptuous dinners to ministers and other politicians, and generally keeps on the right side of the government. They give donations to political leaders and parties for political, 'cultural' or educational purposes. "We should support all, the Congress as well as opposition parties, so that any one who comes to power protects our interests", an office-bearer of the Chamber of Commerce said.[21]

THE URBAN MIDDLE CLASS

The urban middle class largely consists of the upper castes. It is people belonging to the middle class, having increasingly availed themselves of educational opportunities, who get white-collar jobs at various levels in government and semi-government offices, educational institutions, private firms etc. Besides the salaried class, petty shop-keepers, agents and proprietors of small firms, professionals such as doctors, lawyers, journalists etc. form part of the urban middle class. They are from the upper castes.

This middle class feels concerned at the rising unemployment among the educated. Job opportunities in secondary and tertiary sectors have not kept pace with the rise in the number of the educated. It may be noted that the number of colleges in Bihar increased by 283.72 per cent between 1951-52 and 1966-67, whereas primary schools increased by 187.22 per cent. There were 14,079 unemployed graduates in 1967. The number rose to 66,000 in 1972.[22] As elsewhere, the middle class, a majority of which has fixed incomes, had been hard hit by the steep price rise and scarcity of essential commodities.

Sensitive and vocal sections of the middle class had increasingly resorted to direct action to ventilate their grievances. During the period 1967 to 1971, there were 179 agitations in Patna, out of which 110, i.e. 59 per cent of the total number, were launched by government or semi-government employees.[23] School and college teachers also organized processions and demonstrations in Patna. Their demands were mainly for better service conditions including more allowances, job security, and an end to retrenchment.

STUDENTS

Students of Bihar belong to the same upper castes as the middle class. Most of them are sons and daughters of white-collar employees, businessmen and small and big land-holders. Except in the matter of sex relationship and dress style, students have hardly any attitudes and values different from their parents.[24] They are, of course more militant : 26 per cent of the student agitations, as against 9 per cent of the agitations launched by government employees, turned violent.[25]

Caste is a predominant factor on the university campuses of Bihar. Conflicts between students of two different castes are frequent. More often than not, such conflicts culminate in violence. According to one study, casteism and material deprivation—inadequate hostel and transport facilities—were mainly responsible for "whatever was wrong" in the campus of the Patna University.[26] Most of Patna University students strongly felt that teachers and students formed cliques, and that all the decisions of educational institutions, such as appointments of teachers and examiners, admissions, and examination results were made by these cliques.[27] The study further points out that the activists among students did not have much faith in "democratic ways" of getting grievances redressed, they preferred demonstrations, strikes and gheraos to negotiations.[28]

Student unrest in post-independence Bihar can be traced back to 1956 when they clashed with the bus transport authority. It was a violent clash in which two students lost their lives in police firing. Again, between 1965 and 1967 frequent clashes took place between the government and students. The issues were : reduction of fees, organization of the students' union and a judicial inquiry into police excesses etc.

The student agitations in 1956 and 1965-67 often coincided with the agitations of other groups such as government employees, teachers and political parties; they supported each other. For instance, in August 1965 student riots in Patna occurred on the same day on which an anti-price rise demonstration was organized by political parties. The non-gazetted officers also organized a demonstration on that very day. All the groups supported the call for Patna bandh.[29] Again in October 1966, teachers, lawyers and such other groups participated in students' demonstrations against police firing.

Moreover, localized student riots often spread to other parts of the state. In 1956, student riots which began in Patna spread to many towns of Bihar. Similarly, in 1966 student riots first took place in Muzaffarpur but immediately spread to all urban areas of the state.

Students as a group also actively participated in the elections which followed student unrest. In the 1957 and 1967 elections, students worked against the Congress to defeat erst- whle chief ministers. Students greatly helped the opposition parties in electioneering.

3.   POLITICS IN BIHAR : THE NON-CONGRESS UNITED FRONT (1967 to 1971)

After the third consecutive victory of the Congress in 1962, the oppositition parties became more restive and militant than before ; the number of dharnas, gheraos, processions, fasts and bandhs multiplied. The different political parties and group such as students, government employees and trade unions, organized demonstrations in August 1965. The Samyukta Socialist Party (SSP) gave a call for Patna bandh on August 9. The call was supported by most of the opposition parties and groups. There was a confrontation between the police and crowds of students, government employees and labourers, and violence erupted at several places in Patna. The trouble spread to other towns in Bihar. All prominent party leaders of the SSP and the Communist Par y of India (CPI), altogether numbering 3,386, were arrested and police firings were reported from 23 places.[30]

Following these events, the SSP and the CPI took a lead in forming a united front against the Congress party. The SSP did not have major ideological differences with the Congress, except on industrial policy, but it believed that the Congress was the main obstacle in carrying out socialist policies and that it must be removed from power at all costs. Madhu Limaye, a SSP leader, said that Right consolidation or Left unity was irrelevant to Indian politics. For the SSP what mattered in Indian politics was the removal of the Congress from power at the Centre.

The membership of the SSP in Bihar, loose and fluctuating, stood at 51,526 in 1966. It did not have a disciplined and committed cadre. People joined the party under the influence of some leaders or to agitate for certain issues rather than because of the socialist ideology of the party. The CPI, on the other hand, had only half the number of members (25,462 in 1966), but its membership was stable, and members were disciplined and ideologically committed. It had a more centralized and a more articulate organizational structure.[31] Following the guidelines from the Soviet Union, the CPI believed that there were "progressive elements" in the Congress which needed to be supported.

Some other 'Left' and 'Right' parties like the Revolutionary Socialist Party and Socialist Unity Centre, the Jharkhand Party and the Janata Party, joined the Front. The United Front parties agreed in principle to co-ordinate their activities in the legislature, in public agitations and in the 1967 elections. Partial electoral adjustments took place among the partners. The SSP and CPI got the lion's share of the nominations, 160 and 61 seats respectively.

The Praja Socialist Party (PSP) and the Jana Sangh did not join the Front. Most of the members of the PSP were then thinking of joining the Congress party. The Jana Sangh did not join the Front because it thought that the Front was dominated by the Left parties, particularly the CPI—its enemy number one. The Jana Sangh maintained that "it alone has the tenacity to resist the inroads of communists and that it alone has the organization which can and will challenge the communists, if necessary, at the barricades."[32] Like the CPI, the Jana Sangh was a well organized party. Its members were disciplined and committed to the pary's ideology.

The opposition parties, it may be mentioned, had the blessings of Jayaprakash Narayan. In 1966, he had expressed his concern over the deteriorating condition of the country. He told students in Patna that it would be in the interest of democracy if the Congress lost some states in the 1967 elections. He felt that the ruling party needed a shock treatment.[33]

The Congress failed to secure a majority in the state assembly, securing only 41 per cent of the total number of seats. The United Front formed the government, and was joined by the Jana Sangh which had secured 26 seats. But internal bickerings soon began, defections from one group or party to another increased; ideological differences on issues like the rights of share croppers and the status of Urdu became sharp between the Left and Right parties, particularly the CPI and the Jana Sangh. As a result, between March 1967 and May 1968, four ministries had come and gone. By the end of 1968, the assembly was dissolved.

In February 1969 fresh elections were held. Once again the Congress did not get a majority in the legislature, but the SSP strength declined from 86 in 1967 to 70 seats, owing largely to organizational weakness. On the other hand, the Jana Sangh, with its cohesive organization, improved its strength from 26 to 34 seats. The CPI retained its earlier strength of 28 seats.

The Congress formed a coalition government with the Soshit Dal, the Janata Party and the Jharkhand as partners. The ministry did not continue for more than 77 days. Then the non-Congress United Front came to power. The CPI, the Jana Sangh and the SSP supported the ministry but did not join the government. It ruled for only one year. In all, five ministries were formed between 1969 and 1972. Thus, the instability of 1967-68 was repeated.

The pattern of alliance, however, changed after 1969. The CPI and the Jana Sangh did not join hands. After the Congress split in 1969, the CPI came closer to the ruling Congress. This was followed by an alliance between the two parties in the 1971 Lok Sabha and 1972 Vidhan Sabha elections. On the other side, the SSP, the Congress (O), and the Jana Sangh reached an electoral pact to fight the 1971 Lok Sabha elections. Understandably, these parties were the main constituents of the 1974-75 movement in Bihar.

THE CONGRESS

The Congress call for *Garibi Hatao* and its socialist stance influenced the electorate in the 1972 elections. It secured a majority in the State Assembly, but it got only 33 per cent of the votes, that is, less then what it had got in the 1962 elections. The performance of the Congress government after 1972 remained as poor as in the past. Its socialistic policies did not go beyond nationalization of a few industries and a few inefficiently implemented measures of welfarism.

The Congress was riven with factions. Factional fights were a legacy of the the pre-independence days. The factions, based neither on class interests nor on ideology no politics, centred on personalitses and ran along caste lines. While earlier the struggle between Kayasthas and Bhumihars dominated party affairs, both wooing Rajputs and Brahmins to broaden their respective base, after independence caste alliances changed, and rivalries for ministerial positions within each caste slowly surfaced. During the fifties Kayasthas got isolated, and the midde castes, Ahirs and Kurmis, joined the struggle for power. In the seventies, though the struggle is confined to Bhumihars, Brahmins and Rajputs, the Brahmin faction dominates the Congress.[34] The appointment in 1973 of Abdul Ghafoor as chief minister by the Congress High Command failed to bring about a truce, and in April 1975 Ghafoor was replaced by Jagannath Mishra, a Brahmin.

4. THE REGIME

The Bihar regime was (and, of course con.inues to be) under the control of upper castes-cum-middle classes. In rural areas the landed class dominates the administration. In urban areas power was diffused among different groups. Businessmen and entrepreneurs, professionals (doctors, pleaders, journalists, engineers, teachers etc.), and white-collar employees wielded effective power. Competing politicians, within or outside one's own political party, not only belonged to the same class but most of them consciously upheld their class interests as against the interests of other classes. They isolated anyone, irrespective of the party, who talked about class struggle or organized a class other their own.

Having taken care of their own class interests, politicians fought for political power for personal gain. Political positions provided them with opportunities to raise their own as well as their kinsmen's social and economic status. For achieving, holding and advancing their power, they resorted to manipulation. They appealed for caste solidarity and similar primordial sentiments to get votes. They used propaganda and organizational skill, money, might and patronage to win elections. Capturing of polling booths and indulging in bogus voting by all parties were not uncommon in Bihar.

Having acquired power, they tried to maintain it by hook or by crook. They used their positions to oblige their supporters. In so doing they often violated the accepted rules of the game of the present political system. Corruption in Bihar was rampant : a minister took a bribe of Rs. 1,75,000 from a contractor; a son of a chief minister used 500 acres of government land for ten years without paying rent or compensation; tenders of one company were accepted over those of others because it paid money or because the owner belonged to the minister's or secretary's caste or kin group; ministers entered into shady transactions with firms. The Aiyar and Mudholkar Commission reports are full of details of similar corrupt practices of ministers both of the Congress and of the United Front. A.G. Noorani observes, "It was a naked struggle for power with no holds barred and with each faction regarding public office as a means of furthering its own position. Charges of corruption, nepotism and plain abuse of power were freely bandied about."[35]

The administrators are not much interested in carrying out their duties. They find their work thankless, 'frustrating' and 'pointless'[36]. Corruption among them was the rule. There was a general feeling in Bihar that one cannot get things done — getting fertilizer or seeds or electricity, filing a petition in court, getting admission to hospital, getting admission to schools or colleges, even reserving seats in railway trains—without bribes. Corruption also prevailed in semi-government and voluntary organizations including Sarvodaya institutions.[37] The members of the middle class who were vocal about corruption admitted that they were not above board.

To sum up. First, tensions prevailed among different occupational groups which benefited from the developmental programmes of the last two decades—rich and neo-rich farmers, and urban middle class. Landless agricultural labourers, whose ranks had swollen because of the sale of land by the small and marginal farmers and who had been neglected by all political parties, started raising their voice.

Secondly, political power in Bihar was controlled by the landowing and business classes and industrialists. They were in the Congress, (O), Jana Sangh and Swatantra party. The neo-rich

farmers and urban white collar employees influenced government's decisions and their implementation without *overtly*
possessing political power. The interests of these groups were not
the same as those of the agricultural labourers, marginal
farmers, factory workers and casual labourers.

Thirdly, most political leaders having secured their
interests. resorted to manipulative politics to get power. In so
doing, even basic rules of the game of the present political
system were ignored or violated.

NOTES

1. S.R. Bose, *Economy of Bihar*, Calcutta, K. L. Firma Publications 1971.
2. Jayaprakash Narayan, A Manifesto for Bihar, *The Sunday Standard*, May, 11, 1975.
3. See, Harry W. Blair, Ethnicity [and Democratic Politics in India, Caste as a Differential Mobilizer in Bihar, *Comparative Politics*; October 1972.
4 Agricultural Labour Enquiry, Ministry of Labour, Government of India, *Rural Manpower and Occupational Structure*, New Delhi, The Manager of Publications, 1954.
5. *Bihar Through Figures*, 1970, Patna, Directorate of Statistics and Evaluation Bihar, 1971.
6. Bose, op. cit.
7. R.N. Maharaj, Survey of Peasant Organization : *A Case Study of Kisan Sabha in Bihar*, (mimiographed) Patna, A.N.S. Institute of Social Studies, 1974.
8. Quoted in JP's Real Mission. *Economic and Political Weekly*. March 22, 1975.
9. Shashishekhar Jha, *Political Elite in Bihar*, Bombay, Vora & Co,. Publishers Pvt. Ltd., 1972.
10. Ibid.
11. Ibid.
12. G.K. Prasad, *Bureaucracy in India : A Sociological Study*, New Delhi, Sterling Publishers Pvt. Ltd., 1974.
13. Maharaj, op. cit.
14. Quoted by Wolf Ladejinsky, New Ceiling Round and Implementation Prospects, *Economic and Political Weekly*, Review of Agriculture, September 30, 1972.
15. Wolf Ladejinsky, Green Revolution in Bihar. The Kosi Area : A Field Trip, ibid., September 27, 1969.
16. Ibid.
17. Maharaj, op. cit.
18. Quoted by Ajit Roy. *Economics and Politics of Garibi Hatao*, Calcutta,

Naya Prakashan, 1973.

19. JP's Real Mission, op. cit.
20. *The Indian Nation*, September 2, 1974.
21. Interview.
22. D.D. Guru, Educated Unemployed and Small Industries, *The Economic Times*, January 13, 1975.
23. A.P. Sinha, *Agitational Behaviour in a State Capital : A Case Study of Patna*, Delhi, Centre for the Study of Developing Societies, 1974 (typescript).
24. See K.D. Gangrade *Inter-Generational Difference: A Study in the Generational Gap*, Delhi, Delhi School of Social Change (*mimeographed*); B.V. Shah, *Social Changes and College Students of Gujarat*, Baroda, The M.S. University of Baroda, 1974. See for further discussion my paper on The Upsurge in Gujarat, *Economic and Political Weekly*, Special Number, August, 1974.
25. Sinha op, cit.
26. Sudha Rani Sinha, *Study of the Effect of Anomic and Alienation on Campus Activism*, unpublished Ph.D. thesis, Patna University, 1971.
27. Ibid.
28. Ibid.
29. *The Searchlight*, August 10, 1965. See also Herbert Heidenzeich The Anatomy of a Riot`: A Caste Study from Bihar, 1965, *Journal of Commonwealth Political Studies*. July 1968.
30. Ibid.
31. Paul R. Brass, Radical Parties of the Left in Bihar : A Comparison of the SSP and the CPI, in *Radical Politics in South Asia* (ed.) Paul R Brass and Marcus F. Franda, Massachusetts, The MIT Press, 1973.
32. Craig` Baxter, *Jana Sangh : A Biography of an Indian Political Party*, Philadelphia, University of Pennsylvania Press, 1969.
33. *The Indian Nation*. October 13, 1966.
34. Ramashray Roy, Caste and Political Recruitment in Bihar, Rajni Kothari (ed), *Caste in Indian Politics*, New Delhi, Orient Longman 1970.
35. *Ministers' Misconduct*, Delhi, Vikas Publishing House, Second Edition, 1974.
36. Prasad, op. cit.
37. Laxminarayan Lal, *Jayaprakash*. (Hindi) Delhi, Macmillan, 1974.

2

Antecedents of the Movement

The Bihar movement proper, which is the subject of this study began after March 18, 1974; but it was only a culmination of certain developments in different parts of rural and urban Bihar. They have a bearing on the nature and direction of the movement. In this chapter we shall discuss these developments and events.

1. AGRARIAN UNREST

Agrarian tensions had been mounting since the late sixties. In the year 1970, there were 649 agrarian agitations, seven times more than in the previous year.[1] The Naxalites and other Left political parties were mobilizing poor peasants and landless labourers against landlords; and clashes between the two were frequent. In June 1973, about 5,000 people, mostly landless labourers and poor peasants carrying CPI banner, attacked the house of a farmer in Ghorbanki village in south Bihar. They took away all that he had in cash and kind. It is reported that 70 bighas of his land were grabbed by the agitators. *The India Nation* noted that, "Ghorbanki is only one in hundreds of such cases. In all, about 15,000 cases out of agrarian troubles are pending disposal in the district."[2]

2. URBAN UNREST

In the towns, teachers, government employees, and other sections of the vocal urban middle class raised their voice against sky-rocketing prices and increasing hardships. The imposition of professional tax in 1973 added fuel to the fire. The

state government imposed the tax on anyone having an income
of Rs. 300 per month. Needless to say, this affected not only
the middle class but also the working class. The opposition
parties and trade unions formed an organization known
as Bihar Rajya Mahgai Abhaab Pesha Kar Virodhi Mazdur
Swa Karmachari Sangharsh Samiti (the Bihar State struggle
committee of labourers and employees to oppose price rise
and professional tax) to launch a struggle against the imposition of the tax. The Committee was dominated by the CPI
and other Left parties.

The Committee organized "massive" rallies before the
Vidhan Sabha on December 16, 1973 against high prices, non-
availability of essential commodities, and imposition of the
professional tax. More than 120 trade unions, including
those of industrial workers, teachers, engineers, journalists,
government and university employees, railwaymen etc.,
participated in the demonstration. The main slogan of the
procession was : *Pura Rashan Pura Kam, Nahito Hoga Chakka
Jam* (full ration to ensure full work or else all work would
come to a grinding halt). The demonstrators were addressed
by the trade union leaders of different political parties including the CPI and the Jana Sangh.

Again, the Samyukta Sangharsh Samiti (the united struggle
committee) of the CPI, CPM, SSP, Jana Sangh and other
splinter groups gave a call for Bihar bandh on January 21,
1974 to protest against high prices and scarcity of essential
commodities. The bandh was supported by nearly 400 trade
unions.

A small section of the Jana Sangh party had reservations
about the bandh call. The Akhil Bharatiya Vidyarthi Parishad
(ABVP), a pro-Jana Sangh student organization, did not
support the bandh. However, the Jana Sangh organized an
independent procession in Patna to support the bandh against
price-rise. The CPI volunteers burnt the effigies of the Prime
Minister and the Chief Minister and shouted slogans against
them. A dominant section of the Congress leaders, thanks to
their internal power struggle, did not take note of anti-Chief
Minister slogans. But the anti-Prime Minister slogans were
sharply criticized by Sitaram Kesari, the President of the Bihar
Congress, who said, "Our friends have joined hands with

reactionary parties like SSP, Jana Sangh and Congress (O)."[3]

On the day of the bandh on 21 January 1974, educational institutions and the markets remained closed. The buses of the Road Transport Corporation did not run. Clashes between the administrative authority and demonstrators took place at a few places like Ranchi, Begusarai, Gaya, Kathiya, Motihari, and Jahanabad. In Patna, a few foodgrains shops were looted by a mob. Police firing took place at Koderma railway station.

3. STUDENTS' AGITATION

Simultaneously, student agitation relating to amenities on campuses, reduction in fees, concession in cinema tickets etc. erupted in Patna and other towns. Patna students hijacked two State Transport buses on December 5, 1973. Clashes between students and Road Transport authority continued for a few days. On December 10, several hundred students of the Patna University, of the Homeopathic College along with non-teaching employees of the Patna University and Anand Margis held demonstrations before the secretariat. The police fired 17 rounds of tear-gas shells to disperse the demonstrators. Thereafter sporadic strikes and demonstrations of students continued in some parts of the state.

Meanwhile, particularly after the anti-price rise demonstration of December 16, the leaders of ABVP of Bihar were planning to launch a state-wide agitation that would exclude the communists. They discussed the plan at a conference in Dhanbad. The ABVP, it may be mentioned, had gained ground in the university campuses after 1972, defeating the CPI's All India Students Federation (AISF). Following the conference, the ABVP organized a three-day camp of student leaders in early January at Muzaffarpur to evolve a strategy for the agitation. The organisers invited the student leaders of the Samajwadi Yuvajana Sabha (SYS) of the SSP but not those of the student fronts of the CPI and the CPM.

The ABVP leaders considered Jayaprakash to be best suited to guide the non-communist agitation. Jayaprakash Narayan himself was thinking of a student movement. He took the opportunity in the third week of December to address a meeting of students at Muzaffarpur, arranged by the supporters of the ABVP. JP appealed to the students to give up their studies for a year to "save democracy". On the eve of the Bihar bandh against price rise on January 21, which, as mentioned above, was not supported by the ABVP, JP declared that the Marxian order did not suit this country.[4] Enthused by this formulation of JP's, the ABVP-dominated Patna University Students' Union invited him to preside over the symposium on "Youth For Democracy" on 22 January. It may be mentioned that the Sarvodaya youth front, the Tarun Shanti Sena (TSS), which was taken as a co-sponsor had hardly ten members in the University. Jayaprakash called upon the students to take a few days' leave from their universities and go to villages where people belonging to lower strata of society were not allowed to exercise their right of franchise. He said that students were the only people who could do this successfully. If they did not come forward, democracy was bound to prove a failure in the country. JP reminded them that by-elections were going to be held at Madhubani and Kunti, and added, "I hope my voice would reach the student community at these two places and they would do the needful."[5]

On another occasion, at a meeting, again organized by Patna University Students' Union and Tarun Shanti Sena, JP said that the existing pattern of education was "defective and outdated." He invited students to take part in national politics without falling a prey to party politics. He appealed to the students to give a new direction to politics and to safeguard democracy in India.

Similarly, K.B. Sahay, a former Chief Minister and a Congress (O) leader, gave a spirited call to the youth to come forward in large numbers and take over from the older generation the responsibility of reconstructing the country.[6] Karpoori Thakur, another ex-Chief Minister and SSP MLA, appealed to the opposition parties, intellectuals, students, and youth to declare a 'jehad' (crusade) on the pattern of Gujarat for ending "the Congress misrule" in Bihar.[7]

Having created an atmosphere for the agitation, the leaders of the ABVP were poised for action. Under their leadership, but in collaboration with the TSS, students of Muzaffarpur organized a procession against price rise in the town on February 12. It turned violent and the mob smashed the windscreen of three trucks. The agitators also set fire to an empty bullock cart. Again on February 16, the students staged a demonstration demanding reduction in price of text books and concession in cinema tickets. They also formed a flying squad to check the distribution of essential commodities, exhorting all sections of people to remain vigilant against "black marketeers, hoarders and administrators". The CPI workers of Muzaffarpur also organized an anti-price rise rally on February 26 before the District Magistrate's office.

An open confrontation between the students of ABVP and CPI took place in the third week of February 1974. The students of SYS and TSS were inclined towards the former rather than towards the latter. The Patna University Students Union organized a conference on February 17 and 18. Its main purpose was to plan a Gujarat-type agitation in Bihar, but the conference split on two resolutions. The pro-ABVP section emphasized the need for *Bharatiya* education, and demanded that India maintain 'equal distance in relations' with Russia and America. The CPI students walked out. Thereafter, the conference formed the Bihar Chhatra Sangharsh Samiti (BCSS) to wage an organized struggle for their demands, which included the lowering of prices of essential commodities, reduction in tution fees, availability of cheap books, students participation in university management, *Bharatiya* education etc.

The leftist students organized a separate conference on February 26 and 27. Its demands were, *inter alia*, supply of foodgrains and other essential commodities at subsidized rates, unemployment allowance to the educated unemployed youth and establishment of students' union in all colleges. The conference formed the Bihar Chhatra Naujawan Sangharsh Morcha (BCNSM), and decided to organize demonstrations before the Assembly on April 5. Thus, both the student groups, communist and non-communist, started separate preparations to mobilize students in favour of their agitation.

On March 2, the Gandhi Peace Foundation and Tarun Shanti Sena of Muzaffarpur called a meeting of businessmen, officials, students and youth to fix prices of essential commodities. It did not go beyond fixing the price of vegetable oil, and even this was not enforced for long. The students then formed the Chhatra Yuva Manch to check prices. The Manch called a meeting of officials and businessmen on March 13 and again on March 16. The representatives of business demurred at the price list of essential commodities prepared by the students. The leaders of the Chamber of Commerce did not attend the meeting. Businessmen did not turn up for the next meeting, and the officials came late. Thus was the stage set for a confrontation between students and businessmen. The students formed flying squads to check prices.[8]

In Bhagalpur city, at the initiative of the Tarun Shanti Sena a Chhatra Sangharsh Samiti (CSS) was formed. It organized two processions, one on February 6 and the other on February 12. It also passed a resolution that the CSS of Bhagalpur would launch direct action if the government did not take steps to ensure one full meal every day to every citizen, uninterrupted supply of diesel, coal, and vegetable oil, and reduction in bus fare etc.

In Patna, the students of Anugraha Narayan College took out a procession and paraded on the main streets of the town on March 1. Their demands included immediate removal of the college principal, formation of students' union, and a complete change in the present system of education. On March 13, the students of Bihar University set fire to the University building. They demanded the postponement of the dates of M.A. and M.Sc. examinations as classes had not been held for a full session.

In protest against the government's closure of Patna University, about 200 students raided the University office on March 14. They forced out the Vice-Chancellor, officers and staff of the University, seized the keys and locked up all the the doors, and proclaimed V.N. Singh, 'a senior member' of of the BCSS, as their Vice-Chancellor. A similar incident took place in a college in Patna : at a meeting students dissolved the existing managing committee, suspended the principal and vice-principal, and appointed two students in their places.

On March 4, the BCNSM gheraoed the District Magistrates of Patna, Barh, Fatwah and Mokameh. They demanded that the authorities concede the pending demands of the Homeopathic, Ayurvedic, I.I.T. and P.N. College students. On that day students hijacked nine buses of the State Transport.

The Youth Congress too organized demonstrations in Chhota-nagpur area against soaring prices, scarcity of essential commodities, mounting unemployment and "rampant corruption, blackmarketing, hoarding and profiteering". At places, processions and demonstrations took a violent turn. At Motihari, for instance, the students raided and ransacked the railway station and the telephone exchange.

The events of February and early March 1974 were a clear index of widespread unrest in Bihar. *The Indian Nation* commented :

Leaving them (people) to the care of frustration and hunger is neither socialism nor capitalism. The Government ought to realise that the instinct for survival is compelling many of them to resort to extremist measures. What is happening at present may be just a rehearsal of what may come on a bigger scale in the near future, if the government takes no step to prevent catostrophe.[9]

Forewarned by the Gujarat agitation and the sporadic riots in Bihar, Chief Minister Abdool Ghafoor took some measures to check corruption. Some officers against whom there were charges of misappropriation, favouritism and nepotism were suspended, dismissed or forced to retire. He took steps to provide adequate supply of foodgrains to hostels and student messes. The Chief Minister said that arrangements were being made for the sale of books, exercise books and other stationary in the university campuses. He declared that the government favoured the formation of students unions in all the colleges of the state.

The students of the BCNSM and BCSS, however, ignored these steps and went ahead with their plans to launch an all-out agitation.

4. THE WATERSHED : 18th MARCH 1974

On March 16, the BCNSM organized processions at Patna, Muzaffarpur, Begusarai, Sahebganj, Motihari and other places to protest against price-rise. Besides other demands, they asked for the closure of universities and colleges for one year, implementation of land reform measures and state take over of the universities. 'Bihar bhi Gujarat banega'

(Bihar will also become Gujarat) was the main slogan. The leaders tried to hand over a memorandum to the Education Minister. When they did not succeed they said, "If no one is ready to hear us, why should we hear anybody? By our agitation we should force the government to concede our genuine demands." The student leaders also felt that there was no way out for them but to organize a "militant struggle," for the removal of "the present anti-people government."[10]

The processionists in Patna and elsewhere clashed with the police. Students threw stones at a newspaper office. They also raided and brick-batted the residence of the Education Minister. The police burst a number of tear-gas shells to disperse the mob. Incidents of police firing and lathi charge were reported from Muzaffarpur and Motihari as well.

The BCSS condemned the brick-batting on the newspaper office. It organized a gherao on March 18, of the Assembly and the Governor to prevent the Governor from addressing the joint session of the Assembly. The contention of the BCSS leaders was that the Governor's address to the joint session was not independent of the policies and opinion of the ruling party, and that since the ruling party did not represent the people's voice, their difficulties and aspirations, the Governor's address was meaningless. The Governor, it was argued, should not become a tool of the ruling party, and should therefore read instead the speech prepared by the BCSS which voiced people's grievances. The Governor, however, did not agree with them.

The BCSS programme for the gherao of the Assembly was jointly sponsored by different student and youth organizations, such as the youth wing of the Congress-O, ABVP, Tarun Shanti Sena, Samajwadi Yuvajana Sabha, Bihar State Students' Council, Bharatiya Krantikari Yuvak Sangh, and Bharatiya Yuva Sangh. The BCNSM did not oppose the 18th March programme, but asked its members and supporters not to participate in it.

In a joint statement, the members of the BCSS, the President of the Patna University Students' Union, Lalu Prasad, and the President of the Bihar Chhatra Parishad, Narendra Singh, warned politicians not to involve the students in the game of power politics. They asked them to keep their hands off in "tomorrow's gherao and demonstration before the Bihar Legislature." They said that politicians would not be allowed to participate in the demonstration because their main object was to gherao the Governor, ministers and MLAs belonging to all political parties. "Our agitation," they said, "is against the high prices, rampant corruption and mounting unemployment among educated youth." Besides other things, they demanded loans to unemployed youth to start small business or small-scale industries and a job-oriented education.

On March 18, several hundred students from Patna and other parts of the state assembled near Raj Bhavan and the state Assembly to prevent the Governor from attending the Assembly. The Governor, however, changed the route and eluded them. But a direct confrontation between the police and students took place near the Assembly. Different groups adopted different methods : one mob set fire to government buildings, another looted posh hotels and godowns of the Food Corporation, yet another broke open six railway wagons and looted mustard and vegetable oil. A mob attacked newspaper offices, and set fire to the offices of the English daily *Searchlight* and the Hindi daily *Pradeep*, both housed in the same building.

There was elaborate police *bandobast*. But the state machinery was thrown completely out of gear, at least for two hours, in other parts of Patna. The city was under almost complete control of the mobs. No protection was provided by authority to newspaper offices, government offices or private buildings. The city was paralysed. *The Indian Nation* expressed the agony in the following words :

"We have no words to describe the situation in which we are reappearing before our readers. Two dailies of the State, *The Searchlight* and *Pradeep* have been destroyed. *The Indian Nation* and *Aryavarta* too would have met the same fate, if their workers had not risked their lives to save them. ... On the 18th March, we coaxed, cajoled, implored and entreated all the high-ups right from the Chief Minister to the District Magistrate to protect us against the hooligans who were making attempt after attempt to destroy us but none could come to our rescue. Finally, we had to convey our plight to the Prime Minister and the Union Home Minister. But even then it took the Bihar Government more

than two hours to post armed constables at our gates.
Inspite of our best efforts, not for once we could establish
contact with the Inspector General of Police or even with
the police officers of lower ranks.

"The Chief Minister of course was available on the
telephone and he had also the courtesy to come down to
our office at midnight to assuage our feelings, but he was
helpless in the matter of providing protection. He says
that he had been repeatedly telling the IG and the DIG to
protect the Press but his orders were not carried out. This
arouses many suspicions in our minds. Had the writ of
the Government ceased to run in the Police Department ?...

"But who had not failed? One day before the opening
of the Assembly session the Chief Secretary told a news
agency that the security arrangements had been tightened
and the army was 'standing by' to deal with any situation
that might arise...

"But they were nowhere to be seen on the 18th March
till a large number of institutions, shops and hotels, had
been burnt and plundered by hooligans. It is said, that the
entire strength of the police was engaged in the more important task of protecting the Governor, the ministers and
legislators."[11]

Why did the administration completely fail to provide protection to newspaper offices and government departments?
Which groups were active in paralysing the city? These questions need a separate study. But it seems certain that the Chief
Minister had no control over the administration. And some
administrators, for whatever reason, were sympathetic to the
demonstrators or were indifferent to the grim situation in
Patna.

The disturbance on 18th March set the ball of agitation
rolling. On the following day riots took place in Ranchi,
Dhanbad, Chhapra, Saharsa, Gaya, Madhepura, Hazaribagh,
Singriaran and Monghyr. Railway stations, post-offices, courts,
state dispensaries and other buildings were the main targets of
attack. In Bhagalpur a bomb was thrown on the fire brigade
office, and two fish-plates on the main railway line between
Mansi and Mahesh Kunt stations were removed. By March 20,

curfew was imposed on eleven towns—Patna, Bettiah, Ranchi, Monghyr, Chhapra, Gaya, Bihar-Sharif, Jahanabad, Bhagaria, Giridih and Chaibasa. The army was called out at several places and ordered to shoot at sight. By March 21, about 22 persons had died in police firings, and several hundred persons had been arrested.

The trouble also spread to rural areas. A village post-office in Jagdishpur was attacked. At Garhan some office papers were destroyed. Two post-offices in Manjhaul village and Negla village were heavily brickbatted. Office records were thrown into a well. Block officers at Hussenabad, Majhiwad and Chainpur were attacked.

To maintain the tempo of the agitation, the BCSS gave a call for Bihar bandh on March 23. Till then Jayaprakash Narayan, though in Patna, had not made any comment on the 18th March incidents. On March 22, he requested the students to reconsider the bandh call, but without success. He feared that the bandh would turn violent, and the BCSS would be held responsible. The bandh however, passed off peacefully.

Political demands—resignation of the Ghafoor ministry and dissolution of the State Assembly—came to be raised on the 23rd. On the eve of the bandh, JP advised Ghafoor to step down because of the "monumental failure of the government to control the situation" on March. 18 Political leaders also joined the stir. Mahamaya Prasad Sinha, a former chief minister called for the resignation of the Ghafoor ministry and the dissolution of the State Assembly. Karpoori Thakur of the SSP supported the students' movement. The students of Madhubani and Motihari submitted a memorandum on March 23, to the Deputy Commissioner demanding the dissolution of Bihar Vidhan Sabha, and asking for a judicial inquiry into police firing at various places in the state. On March 27, the BCSS threatened to launch a movement "to paralyse the government" if the ministry headed by Abdul Ghafoor did not submit its resignation by April 8. Besides, it demanded immediate reopening of the colleges, withdrawal of the police force, unconditional release of all students and payment of compensation to families of the victims of police firing.

The movement continued on the lines of Gujarat agitation. College girls, housewives, lawyers, doctors, teachers, artists and other sections of urban middle class joined the agitation. Different groups organized processions, observed fast or gheraoed government offices and Congress leaders. Simultaneously, violent incidents, such as throwing of bombs, setting fire to public buildings, looting of shops and brick-batting of the police and government offices continued at several places.

On April 6, the President of the Patna University Students' Union and some other student leaders of the ABVP met Sarvodaya leader Jayaprakash Narayan. They requested him to take over the leadership. They assured him that they would abide by his direction and guidance. Jayaprakash, sympathetic to the students, had been watching the events in agony. He felt that he could no longer remain "a silent spectator of misgovernment, corruption and the rest whether in Patna, Delhi or elsewhere"[12]. He agreed to assume the leadership of the mov ment.

On April 8, the Sarvodaya Mandal, Taurn Shanti Sena and Gandhi Peace Foundation organized a silent procession in Patna, led by JP. This gave a new and decisive turn to the agitation. The processionists had gagged themselves and covered their heads with saffron-coloured scarves. A new slogan emphasizing non-violence was raised: *Hamla Chahe Jaisa Hoga Hathen Hamarah Nahi Uthega* (Whatever be the form of attack we shall not raise our hands in retaliation). On the same day, the BCSS performed a *shradh* ceremony for the students killed in police firing at Patna on March 18, and a special prayer in the Vishnu temple; puris and sweets were distributed to over one hundred Brahmins and *daridra narayana*, i.e. poor, according to Hindu custom.

Several programmes such as observing black day, Janata curfew, dharnas, taking out silent processions, torch processions etc. also continued throughout April. Checking prices, unearthing hoarding, distributing essential commodities at fixed prices etc. also continued in some towns of the state. The enthusiasm of the participants was at its peak. It may be added that teachers, engineers, non-gazetted employees etc. were also fighting separately for the redress of their own grievances. This also added to the surging tempo of the agitation

Thus urban unrest of March 1974 overshadowed the rural unrest. Launched by the middle class and working class and led by the Left parties, the leadership of the struggle against price rise and other economic difficulties passed into the hands of students. Subsequently, political demands came to the fore, eclipsing economic demands. Significantly, the Chief Minister's resignation was demanded primarily for his failure to maintain law and order on March 18. Although the urban middle class joined hands with students, the working class kept aloof. The agitation was planned and executed by non-communist parties in general and Right parties and groups in particular, the Left parties and students having been sidelined totally.

NOTES

1. K.C. Pant, Violence In a Period of Social Change; *Young India*, Vol. 3, No. 29-30, 1973.
2. Ibid., July 7, 1973.
3. *The Indian Nation*, February 10, 1974.
4. Ibid., January 21, 1974.
5. Ibid., January 22, 1974.
6. Ibid., February 2, 1974.
7. Ibid., March 3, 1974.
8. *Muzaffarpur me Gandhi Shanti Pratisthan Aur Tarun Shanti Sena ki Bhumika* (Hindi) Patna, Bihar Sarvodaya Mandal, 1974.
9. March 8, 1974.
10. *The Indian Nation*, March 16, 1974.
11. Ibid., March 20, 1974.
12. *Everyman's*, June 1, 1974.

3

The Movement

The upsurge of the urban middle class crystallized in a movement under the leadership of Jayaprakash Narayan more decisively after the events of March. 18 It mobilized hundreds of people, raised several issues and launched many programmes. During the first year of the movement frequent confrontations took place between the agitators and authority. More than one hundred persons died in police firings and several hundreds were injured and many more arrested. On some occasions the state government was paralysed.

The leaders of the movement claimed that it was a revolutionary movement aimed at bringing about total revolution in society. Several questions have, however, still been left unanswered : Was there a philosophy or doctrine underlying and guiding the movement? Did the leadership give it a direction towards revolution? Did the movement have a well-knit organization and a committed cadre? Did JP take the movement forward from the stage it had reached in March 1974? We shall study these aspects of the movement with a view to understanding the nature and direction of the movement. Theaccount is not chronological.

1. ORGANIZATION AND LEADERSHIP

The Bihar Chhatra Sangharsh Samiti (BCSS), a committee of non-communist students, was the central organization of the movement. Its office was located in the Tarun Shanti Sena's (TSS) building in Patna, a few yards away from JP's residence. It coordinated and directed local Chhatra Sangharsh Samitis (CSS). Different student leaders looked after different functions like preparing press notes, sending circulars to local CSSs, attending to correspondence and maintaining office records. It published an irregular weekly known as the *Tarun Kranti*. JP supervised the work of the BCSS through Sarvodaya or TSS workers.

CSSs had been formed in all cities and district head-quarters, in many towns and villages, in colleges and schools. At some places, particularly at the district level, the CSS had an office, mostly housed in Gandhi Peace Foundation build-ings, Sarvodaya offices or Khadi bhandars i.e. shops. Where there were no offices, the residence of a prominent political leader, usually of the Jana Sangh, was used as a meeting place by the CSS leaders. The local CSS carried out the pro-grammes decided by the BCSS, but sometimes formulated its own programmes. Some Samitis published a weekly or a fortnightly.

The links between the local CSS and the central organ-zation were weak. The leaders of the BCSS complained that despite their repeated reminders many CSSs did not give the names of the office-bearers nor send reports of their activities. Many CSSs, on the other hand, complained that they received no 'guidance' from the central office nor were they 'officially' informed of the programmes. It was the Sarvodaya workers who functioned as a link between CSS and the BCSS. They gave either written or oral reports of the activities of CSS to the BCSS. They also conveyed and explained instructions and programmes of the BCSS to the CSSs.

The BCSS was composed of 24 students, sons of govern-ment officers, teachers, businessmen or farmers. An over-whelming number of them (twenty, to be precise) belonged to the upper castes : 9 Rajputs, 4 Bhumihars, 4 Kayasthas, 2 Baniyas and 1 Brahmin. Of the rest two were Ahirs, one a Kurmi and another a Muslim. Thus, the leadership of the BCSS was dominated by upper castes and upper middle classes. It may also be noted that the Brahmins, otherwise very active in Bihar politics, were not deeply involved in this movement because they dominated the Congress party.

Party-wise, one-third of the members of the BCSS belonged to the ABVP, four to the Samajwadi Yuvajana Sabha (SYS), two each to the TSS and the Congress (O), and one to the Chhatra Parishad. Seven leaders were not attached to any party or group. The data on all local CSSs are not available, but the leadership pattern of these was not very much different from that of the central organization.

The student leaders were in no way different from the student leaders in other parts of the country : militant but intellectually not well equipped. Many of them hardly understood JP's philosophy of total revolution. They used high sounding words, often contradicting themselves. They appeared more interested in press publicity and coffee-house gossip than in building up the organization or carrying out the programmes with devotion. In the early stages of the movement the leaders used the funds lavishly till JP first, demanded accounts and subsequently, put certain restrictions on the use of funds, to their great embarrassment. The workers of the TSS were, however, an exception. They were simple, polite and committed to the cause. I found them more upset and anxious than the others that the movement was not progressing fast enough towards the stipulated goal.

Student leaders were more against the Congress than against the political system. To them total revolution was a slogan, not an ideal. Under JP's influence, they talked about Gandhi, non-violence and peaceful revolution, but actually believed that nothing would be attained by non-violence. The initial enthusiasm of some of them waned by the end of the year. I came across a few who were once very enthusiastic about the movement but had begun to doubt the potentiality of the movement for attaining total revolution. They started questioning not only certain assumptions of the movement, but even its direction.

During the course of the movement conflicts among the major groups came to the surface. The leaders of the ABVP made every attempt to dominate the CSSs by giving key positions to the cadre of Rashtriya Swayamsevak Sangh (RSS). At some places they tried to ignore, and even kept out, the CSS workers not belonging to the RSS and Jana Sangh. The ABVP, RSS and Jana Sangh tried to draw non-party boys into their own fold. At some places, the ABVP tried to impress upon them that it was their organization that was carrying on the movement. The TSS and SYS worked as a counterforce to the ABVP, and tried to isolate the ABVP, RSS and Jana Sangh boys. At some places the rivalry went to such an extent that parallel CSSs came into existence.

Jayaprakash, unhappy with the internal quarrels, asked all the office-bearers of the BCSS to submit their resignation so that he could reorganize it. The resignation of the members of the BCSS had been with JP for several months without being accepted. The reorganization of the BCSS remained an unfinished task. He had, however, formed the Chhatra Yuva Sangharsh Vahini. Its members were obliged to make a solemn declaration that they were not members of any political party or its front organizations. The Vahini had enrolled about 800 members by April 1975.

The Bihar Jana Sangharsh Samiti (BJSS), a non-student central organization, was formed after JP took over the leadership of the movement. It was not active beyond occasionally issuing statements to the press. Jana Sangharsh Samitis (JSS) had been formed in most of the towns and some villages, but they were paper organizations. The BJSS was dominated by upper castes and middle class including teachers, writers, lawyers and Sarvodaya workers. Its chapters in towns were dominated by shopkeepers, pleaders and doctors. In villages, they were controlled by rich peasants who, of course were from the upper castes.

2. THE LEADER : JAYAPRAKASH NARAYAN

Jayaprakash Narayan was the leader of the Bihar movement: he provided the philosophical content of the movement, he formulated programmes for action; he guided the struggle, and he controlled it. While taking over the leadership of the movement, he made this clear: "I won't agree to be a leader only in name. I will take the advice of all, of the students, the people, the Jana Sangharsh Samitis. But the decision will be mine and you will have to accept them"[1]. The Bihar movement was also popularly known as "The JP movement'.

The Bihar movement cannot therefore be understood fully without understanding JP. He is a complex person. He is known among both critics and admirers as a moralist, a Marxist, a liberal, a democrat, a humanist, a politician, a saint, a dreamer and so on. It is beyond the scope of this inquiry to deal with all the aspects of JP's personality. What is attempted here is only a brief sketch bringing out those aspects of his make-up that are relevant to the movement.

Jayaprakash Narayan, Kayastha by caste, was born in a UP-Bihar border village in 1902. As student, political leader and Sarvodaya leader, he spent most of his life in Bihar. In response to Gandhi's appeal to leave educational institutions run by an alien government, JP left college in 1921. After a year, he went to the USA and did his M.A. in sociology from the Wisconsin University.

During his stay in America, he was influenced by Marxism and became a Marxist. But he felt revolted at the norms and personal behaviour of his communist friends who nevertheless influenced him intellectually. Their lack of morality (as he saw it) manifested itself in things like neglect of families, in sex relationship, and, above all, in giving primacy to political power.[2] His own moral values, needless to say, were the product of his own socialization in a middle class Kayastha family. Neither then nor later has he clearly analysed his concept of 'morality'.

JP returned to India in 1929. He found Indian communists, under the control of Comintern, not only keeping away from but opposing the freedom movement under the Indian National Congress. They were denouncing Gandhi as "an agent of the bourgeoisie". As a nationalist, JP disagreed with them, though he did not argue with them on this count. To him, Gandhi was the Mahatma, who was fighting for independence, and could never be an agent of one class. Fired as he was by the idea of India's freedom, JP joined the Congress, even though he found much in it to disagree with. Along with other radical Congressmen, he formed the Congress Socialist Party (CSP) within the Congress in 1934. He invited the communists to join the CSP, and some of them did. But their tactics of "unity from below, opposition from above," that is, winning over the ranks and cirticizing the leaders, hurt JP. "JP remained", his biographer writes, "a somewhat shaken Marxist, but he would never trust the Moscow-oriented communists again"[3].

At its first post-World War II conference held at Kanpur in March 1947, the Congress Socialist Party dropped the word Congress from its name and threw its doors open to those who were not members of the Congress. In 1948 the Party severed its connection with the Congress. Although JP was its General Secretary, his conversion to Gandhism had begun. The assassination of Mahatma Gandhi shocked him. He was moved and he felt the need of Gandhi's "spiritual regeneration". Moral values in JP overshadowed his materialistic outlook. He said in March 1948 :

Communalism has been let loose in the country...... Humanity has been uprooted. There have been mass murders. Women have been raped...Corruption is rampant. Blackmarketing has not stopped...

Is everything due to economic inequalities? Is capitalism the only evil? Can we entirely depend upon class struggle ? I do not think so. Economic approach cannot be the only approach...It has a limited appeal...Therefore, I had made an appeal to Shri Aurobindo and Ramana Maharshi to come out of their seclusion and lead the people...[4]

The Socialist Party contested the 1952 elections with high hopes, but was routed; and JP was held responsible for the electoral debacle. One of his close associates charged him with having enfeebled the party by compelling it to give up the sound Marxist principle of class struggle and by striking a personal friendship with Jawaharlal Nehru. This hurt JP very deeply.[5]

JP's estrangement with Marxism went apace. In his own words : "My final break with Marxism, though not with politics, had come during the three weeks' fast at Poona, (undertaken in atonement for his failure in public duty to make the agreement between the trade union he was representing and the government in writing). It was then that the long process of questioning started by the Russian purges came to an end, and it became clear that materialism as a philosophical outlook could not provide any basis for ethical conduct and any incentive for goodness."[6]

When Vinobha entered Bihar in September 1952 for his bhoodan mission, JP joined him. Within a week donation of nearly 7,000 acres of land was announced at JP's meetings. He was thrilled by the response. In 1954 he pledged himself to be a *jeevandani*, i.e. one who had dedicated his life to bhoodan. His break with Maxism was final. JP turned a

Gandhian, a Sarvodayist. In Masani's words, "Sarvodaya is in a way J.P.'s third religion" 7 (The first two being Hinduism and Marxism). Fed up as he was with intra-party squabbles plaguing the Socialist Party, he slowly withdrew himself from it.

Although in 1957 JP left the party, he did not leave politics. He continued publicly to give his opinion on political matters. It may be recalled that JP wanted that the Congress should be defeated in the 1967 elections at least in some states. As his disappointment with the performance of the bhoodan movement mounted by the end of the sixties, and as economic and political crisis became sharp, JP slowly re-entered the political sphere. In July 1972 at a conference of Sarvodaya workers he talked of partyless democracy which was interpreted in the press as a call to his colleagues to return to the mainstream of India's political life. The conference also decided to launch a new journal devoted to political commentary. This led to the publication, beginning in July 1973, of *Everyman's* weekly.[8]

In August 1972 he expressed his fear that power was being concentrated in one hand, in the Prime Minister's. He emphasized the importance of the freedom of the press and the need for a fundamental change in the electoral system. Later, he joined issues with the Congress and the Prime Minister on the question of judiciary's independence and fundamental rights. In his letter to the Prime Minister in June 1973, JP maintained that "unless constitutional safeguards are provided to restrain Parliament from abrogating the fundamental freedom of the citizen except suspending them for temporary periods and in clearly specified circumstances and unless the independence of judiciary is credibly assured, the very foundations of our democracy will be in danger of being totally destroyed."[9] He also raised the issue of corruption in administrative and political life. He wrote a letter to all members of Parliament on these matters, but he did not get any response from them.

Meanwhile, the leaders of the opposition parties persuaded Jayaprakash to try to bring them together so that there could be a viable opposition to the Congress. Extending his moral support, JP met Biju Patnaik and other leaders of opposition parties, but found that they were not ready to sink their differences.[10] He said that without a strong opposition party democracy could not be a success in the country, but the unity he was seeking eluded him.

Encouraged by student revolts in some countries in Europe and Asia, JP came to pin his hopes in the Indian youth as the revolutionary force. In December 1973 he appealed to youth to organize and launch a movement to save democracy. He addressed them thus : "Will our youth continue to look on idly at this strangulation of the democratic process at its very birth? Surely, there cannot be a more important issue which should move the youth to action? Time for action is here and now... It is time for YOUTH POWER in India to enter the national arena and play a decisive role in establishing the primacy of the people and securing their victory over the power of money, falsehood and brute force"[11]. The 1974 student agitation in Gujarat enthused JP. He sensed 'revolution' in it. Speaking to students at Kanpur in February 1974, he said, "The country is fast heading towards a new revolution. There is another 1942 movement in sight to change the course of history"[12].

While, like other Sarvodaya members, Jayaprakash claims that he does not believe in any ideology;he is for Gandhism, minimum government control, village economy, class collaboration etc. He propounds the Sarvodaya philosophy, and is opposed to communism. His non-ideological stance and moral approach, on the one hand,and the compulsion of political mechanism, on the other, led him to take contradictory or ambiguous stands during the course of this movement. Let us cite a few examples. He was against corruption, but at the same time he took support of publicly 'known' corrupt politicians and businessmen, ignoring the suggestion of a sympathiser that he should evolve and announce the movement's own manner of collecting funds. He declared that he was not against Mrs. Gandhi, but also said that as long as Indira Gandhi and the Congress remained in power at the Centre, democracy was in peril. In February 1974, he said in Gujarat that the conservative parties like the Congress (O) and the Jana Sangh were no different from the Congress, but readily accepted their support barely two months later. He did not approve of the manner of selection of candidates for the 1975 state assembly elections by the Janta Morcha, i.e. People's Front in Gujarat, but nevertheless went to Gujarat to campaign for the Morcha. He declared that his mission in Gujarat was to develop political consciousness among the people, but he asked the people of Gujarat to vote blindly for all the candidates of the Morcha. In Gujarat he expressed his sympathy for the stand of the Khedut Samaj (an organization of rich farmers which, incidentally, gave him a purse of Rs. 50,000)[13] on the question of paddy levy, but in Bihar, having found some of his colleagues in favour of the levy, he took no definite stand and advised his followers to act according to their conscience. Such examples can be multiplied. The contradictions arose from his unwillingness to accept the compulsions of politics. He wished that politics should function above social forces.

Be that as it may, what is more important is that the contradictions in JP's attitude created confusion in the rank and file of the movement. They failed to understand what JP wanted to do. Some of them, including Sarvodaya workers, told me that JP was a confused person.

Nevertheless, Jayaprakash is a charismatic leader. His escape from Hazaribagh jail in 1942 for organizing a violent struggle against British Raj made him a hero of the Indian youth. The role of the Sarvodaya leader in the surrender of the dacoits of the Chambal Valley was hailed by many. His concern for the poor, his moral stance, his simplicity and humility, all contribute to his charisma. He attracted large crowds wherever he went. There was no one in Bihar— among the Sarvodaya workers, political leaders and students —who enjoyed so much influence and command over the movement as JP did. JP made every attempt to keep the movement within the framework of Sarvodaya ideology, both in its objective and in the programmes.

3. OBJECTIVE : TOTAL REVOLUTION

After 5 June, 1975, Jayaprakash Narayan announced "total revolution" as the ultimate objective of the movement, an "all round Revolution,"[14] that, is, social, economic, political, moral and cultural revolution. "This struggle," he said, "is

not for any petty or small aim. It is a revolutionary movement." He emphasized the "internal and external change,
changing the entire social frame from within and also from
the outside, individuls as well as institutions."[15]

The society that JP and Sarvodaya workers envisage is
a Sarvodaya society—non-exploitative, casteless and classless.
The social, economic, political, and cultural frame of such a
society is the Gandhian or Sarvodaya frame. We shall discuss in detail the Sarvodaya philosophy in the next chapter.
Here we shall only note that the basic postulate of Sarvodaya
philosophy is the purity of means.

JP did not give the blueprint of that society ; nor did he
outline the various stages of revolution. Instead, he gave
a long list of proposals: agricultural development, equitable
landownership ; application of appropriate technology to
agriculture such as improved labour-intensive tools and
gadgets, development of domestic and rural industries and
the widest possible spread of small industries, regional planning and development, political and administrative decentralization radical educational reform to destroy its elitist
character ; dismantling the hierarchical caste structure of
Hindu society, dismantling also of the economic hierarchical
structure in a manner that did not discourage production and
create a privileged class of managerial bureaucracy linked
with the political and administrative structure.[16] He, however,
did not spell out how land was to be redistributed or how the
social and economic hierarchy was to be abolished.

4. THE ISSUES

The objectives of the movement were derived from the
various issues which gave rise to the agitation. New issues
were added from time to time ; some were highlighted and
some pushed into the background. In this section we shall
deal with the major issues around which the movement began
and developed.

PRICE RISE

It was the economic issue that had triggered the agitation.

People in general, and urban middle class in particular, felt that traders and industrialists exploited consumers by charging arbitrary prices, by hoarding and black-marketing essential commodities. People found through experience that scarcity affected only those who could not afford to pay high prices. They demanded unearthing of hoarded commodities and ensuring equitable distribution of essential commodities at fixed prices. The government and its officers were accused of protecting the black-marketeers and hoarders. There were protest demonstrations and sporadic rioting.

Jayaprakash Narayan held the government rather than traders and industrialists responsible for the economic hardship of the people. According to him, businessmen were compelled to sell things at higher prices because of the government's rules and controls. The government thus became the sole target of the agitation, which thus became completely political.

Educational Problems

Most of the demands of students during the early phase of the agitation, and even for a while thereafter, were concerned with 'educational problems'. These were of two types. One set of demands related to students' future after they had ceased to be students. They demanded employment-oriented education, assurance of employment, unemployment allowance, provision of bank loans to the educated unemployed for starting industries etc. The other type of problems was related to educational facilities. Students demanded increase in the number of scholarships, and supply of books, stationary, food etc. at cheaper prices. They also demanded provision for proper hostel accommodation; representation of students in policy making bodies of the universities such as the Senate, the Syndicate and the Academic Council; establishment of students' union in every college; decentralization of examinations; removal of percentage restrictions for Inter Science students appearing in competitive examinations for admission to medical colleges; combining of marks in written papers and practicals etc. To these demands was added the demand for concessional rates in bus fare and cinema tickets.

Without commenting on the above demands, Jayaprakash

said that the existing pattern of education was "defective and outdated". After completing the studies, what the students got, at the most, was "security of bondage"[17]. As against the students' demand, the moralist JP believed in delinking education altogether with emyloyment. He observed, "I have been appalled to find that only a small percentage of our students today are charged with such desire (the desire for knowledge). The rest want nothing more than a degree, which is prized not for its educational but commercial value. A degree for most students is a mere passport to employment. Guardians and parents too have the same attitude towards education and degrees". He appealed to all to discard such an attitude. According to him, "the first requirement of a better and more meaningful education is the presence among young men and women of a sincere desire for knowledge and skills."[18]

CORRUPTION

The problem of corruption had been raised frequently in the past. Mahamaya Prasad Sinha made it one of the principal issues in the 1967 elections against the Congress. Thereafter, students frequently demanded action against corrupt ministers and administrators. JP made it the central issue of the movement. "If it is not checked", JP warned, "the whole country will be drowned in the bog of corruption"[19]. The Sarvodaya leader believed that "neither economic development nor social equality is possible if corruption is not rooted out. It is not merely an ethical question though that is important. No nation can exist very long without morality in its conduct, in its political and public life. It touches the very bread of the people. Crores and crores of rupees have gone down the drain in the sense that what is meant for development, the welfare of the people, have gone into the pockets of corrupt people."[20] Political corruption, in his view, was the worst form of corruption because it bred many other forms. According to him, the Central government was the Gangotri, the fountainhead, of corruption.[21] JP assured the business community that the movement was not aimed at them because it did not believe that businessmen were responsible for corruption.[22] The movement was against the government because it was the licence-

and-quota policy of the government which, by forcing them to give money to politicians, made them corrupt.

This was a view which was not shared by all the followers of JP. I asked about 50 students and teachers from different parts of Bihar to define corruption. An overwhelming number of them said that hoarding, blackmarketing and economic exploitation were corruption just like bribe-taking by officia's and politicians. Some of them doubted if corruption could be ended by removing the Congress from power.

DEMOCRACY

After the 1972 state assembly elections Jayaprakash Narayan repeatedly said that democracy was in danger in India. He felt that "behind the facade of democracy the country is slowly moving towards dictatorship".[23] During the course of the movement, he often accused the ruling Congress party and the Prime Minister of working for dictatorship. He protested against the repressive measures taken to curb the movement and asserted that it was a fundamental right to speak, to assemble and to hold demonstrations in a democracy. JP and his colleagues felt that the weakening of democracy in the country had reached the point where the mechanism of self-correction had completely broken down :[24] and politcal parties cared only for their power and not for the people, and the people, lacked political consciousness. It was therefore necessary, he said, to develop *Jana Shukti*, people's power. In the next chapter we shall discuss the concept in more detail.

In the existing political system inequality of representation was striking. In 1962, for instance, castes accounting for 30 per cent of the state's population had no representation at all in legislature. Similarly, 26 per cent of the castes went unrepresented in 1967. Low castes were used by political parties as mere vote 'banks' controlled by money power. JP said that must end.[25] He wanted that the electoral system should be changed radically. Under the present electoral system, "the unlimited use of money, large scale impersonation, use of force to prevent the weakest sections from exercising their franchise, abuse of the electoral machinery, hood-winking of the people, particularly the poor and unsophisticated by making attractive but fals promises etc., have robbed the elections of much of their value and eroded the people's faith in them. If this loss of faith deepens and persists, we would soon have a dictatorship in this country"[26]. He wanted the elections to be made genuinely free by curbing money power : "Election expenses should be curtailed if you want that a poor candidate, a peasant or a worker may contest selections, a party of the poor may set up its candidates"[27]. In the selection of candidates, people should have a dominant role in a constituency. He also wanted that after being elected the representative should be responsible to the constituents. To this end he suggested the inclusion of the right to recall in the electoral law.

DISSOLUTION OF THE ASSEMBLY

Jayaprakash Narayan categorically said that he was ready to talk with the Prime Minister or the Congress President on any issue except on the dissolution of the state Assemby   He demanded the resignation of the Ghafoor ministry because it had failed to maintain law and order in Patna on March 18, 1974. After the police firing at Gaya in the first week of April, JP said, "The Assembly by endorsing the Government's repressive measures became a symbol of dishonesty. It gave an apparent popular sanction to the government which the people would never endorse.[25]. He dubbed the Assembly the source of "all the sins that the government has comitted. The Assembly supports them. That's why the ministry must go. The Assembly must go."[29] The Assembly, JP argued, was not performing its functions, the Congress High Command having reduced it "to an unnecessary, burdensome and costly farce."[30] It did not legislate, but had instead abdicated its legislative function to the executive which ruled the state with the help of ordinances. In one single year as many as 176 ordinances were promulgated. Moreover, despite mounting opposition to administrative and political corruption, the state Assembly, instead of taking any step to fight administrative and political corruption had "upheld the corruption and inefficiency and misdeeds of the government." The ruling party MLAs had not fulfilled the promises that they gave to the electorate in the 1972 elections. Therefore, JP said, "Bihar MLAs have no moral and political authority to represent their constituents."[31] They had become anti-people. They should therefore go to the people once again and seek their votes.

JP asserted that the right to call for the dissolution of the assembly was the essence of democracy. He quoted Dicey to argue that people were the political sovereign, the supreme power, and that therefore, they had the right to ask for the dissolution of the Assembly.[32]

Thus the agitation which began on economic and educational issues gradually turned political. During February and March 1974, JP's theme was 'Save Democracy' (though it did not find spontaneous favour among students). Later, issues like political corruption and dissolution of the Assembly became paramount. It may be noted that although complete agreement between JP and the students on the nature and causes of some of the issues was not there, there was no disagreement on the question of the dissolution of the Assembly.

5. PROGRAMMES

Several programmes were launched during the first year of the Bihar movement. They can be classified into three groups (1) Mobilizing programmes—to mobilize the masses for creating and sustaining the tempo of the movement. (2) Issue-oriented programmes—to pressurize or attack some authority or group in relation to some issue or issues. (3) Cadre-building programmes—to recruit and train cadre. Whereas the mobilizing programmes were mainly concerned with expressing the discontent of the people, the issue-oriented programmes were concerned with compelling the authority to act in a particular manner.

The Bihar Chhatra Sangharsh Samiti laid down the programmes and called upon the local Chhatra Sangharsh Samitis and Jana Sangharsh Samitis to implement them. But since different groups had linked themselves with the movement for different purposes, the local programmes differed from place to place and from group to group.

MOBILIZING PROGRAMMES

The mobilizing programmes included organizing processions and demonstrations, rallies, meetings, distributing literature, and undertaking fast.

Two state-wide processions of workers and white-collar employees had been organized in December 1973 and January 1974. They had raised economic issues. But the Bihar movement began with the March 18 procession. Students were the main participants in these, and they voiced the student problems. In the first year of the movement, there were three major processions, on June 5, and on November 4, 1974, and on March 18, 1975. They were massive, their strength varying from fifteen to fifty thousand. But it is worth noting that each successive procession was smaller in size. On the first anniversary of the movement, 18 March, 1975, the procession was almost half the size of the previous one.

On June 5, about half a million people marched from Gandhi Maidan to Raj Bhawan to express their lack of confidence in the State Assembly. The procession, led by Jayaprakash Narayan, submitted a truckload of memoranda with about ten million signatures and thumb impression of voters demanding the dissolution of the Assembly. It was reported that several thousand people were prevented by the authorities from joining the demonstrations. What is more important, shots were fired at the demonstration from a private building. It was alleged that the miscreants belonged to the 'Indira Brigade', a supposedly pro-Congresss militant organization. Twenty-one persons were injured by the shots. Yet the participants remained peaceful, faithful to their pledge that whatever the form of attack they would not raise their hands in retaliation.

On November 4, 1974 the BCSS and BJSS planned to organize a procession and gherao the ministers to demand their resignation. The government took all measures to frustrate the programme. Barricades were put up in and around the town upto a radius of about 30 miles to prevent people from joining the programme; fifty-eight trains on the Eastern Railway were cancelled, all steamers on the Ganga and several state transport buses stopped plying; a number of private vehicles and public carriers were also impounded by the government. Air-borne officers kept a vigil all over the state, sending wireless instructions to the control room on the ground. About 3,000 persons had been arrested by the evening of November 3.

Despite all the repressive measures, about 40,000 people—mainly students and youth, Sarvodaya workers and members of political parties—participated in the procession which, led by Jayaprakash Narayan, started from Gandhi Maidan. It broke police cordon after cordon, barricade after barricade to reach the secretariat. Police burst several rounds of tear-gas shells and resorted to both mild and severe lathi charges at a number of places to stop the processionists. Jayaprakash himself received a lathi blow on his head ; the second blow aimed at him was taken on his arm by Nanaji Deshmukh, the Jana Sangh secretary, the next was stopped by Baburao Chandavar, a Sarvodaya worker. JP's followers formed a human cordon around him. His eyes and throat were affected by teargas. Yet, JP along with the processionists managed to reach the secretariat. There, excepting JP, all others including Jana Sangh and Congress (O) leaders were rounded up. JP followed his followers to the police van to court arrest.

All the three processions focussed on one political issue : dissolution of the Assembly. Out of the 25 slogans prescribed for June 5 procession, 11 were of a political nature, 6 related to government repression, 2 concerned corruption, 2 slogans were of an economic nature (against price rise), 2 demanded changes in the education system, and 2 asked people to be ready to fight and sacrifice. On November 4, seven slogans were prescribed by the BCSS, none concerning economic issues. For the first time a slogan was addressed to the police : "The policeman is our brother; we are not fighting against him."[33] Similar slogans were repeated at the March 18, 1975 procession.

After March 18, 1975, as has been already noted, various groups such as pleaders, teachers and artists organized processions in support of the movement. The local CSS organized morchas or demonstrations before the collectorate in their respective towns. The number of such local processions decreased significantly after December 1974.

August 15, 1974 was observed as Lok Swarajya Day and January 26, 1975 was celebrated as People's Republic Day. On both the occasions different CSSs and JSSs organized separate flag-salutation programmes. At some places flags were hoisted by rickshaw pullers. At some places police prevented students from unfurling the national flag.

Anti-Repression Day or Black Day was observed on August 23 and November 11 against police atrocities. Black flags were hoisted on some buildings, and students, youth, members of political parties and Sarvodaya workers wore black badges. JP appealed all to observe a dawn-to-dusk fast, and did it himself in Patna alongwith a batch of about 180 followers. In July and September, groups of satyagrahis went on fast in front of the Assembly gate, demanding the dissolution of the Assembly. The programme of fasts and flag salutation kept the students active, but did not attract the masses.

Most of the processions and fasts ended with public meetings. Meetings were also held on the eve of, as well as at the end of the bandhs and gheraos. The purpose was to explain to the people the issues involved in the movement, and also to issue instructions regarding future programmes. Jayaprakash Narayan addressed most of the meetings in Patna and in district and taluka towns. He invariably attracted large crowds. On June 5 and November 12, his meetings at Gandhi Maidan in Patna were attended by about one million people. JP generally spoke for two hours. Several political leaders, such as Vajpayee, Advani, Limaye, Karpoori Thakur, and Mahamaya Prasad Sinha also addressed meetings in different districts of Bihar. During April and May 1974, student leaders and Sarvodaya workers organized street corner meetings in cities. They explained the need for and purpose of the movement. The programme of meetings did not continue for long because there were not many speakers, nor were all the speakers intellectually equipped to deal with all kinds of questions raised by the audience.

Leaflets, generally issued by the BCSS and local CSSs, and JSSs, were the common means of communicating programmes, instructions and JP's appeals. They also explained the aims and objectives of the movement, the role of the Congress and the CPI. A content analysis of the available handbills suggests that during March and April 1974 economic problems like price rise and inequality were highlighted, followed by the prevalence of corruption. After May the order was reversed. In fact, the economic problems had almost disappeared in the leaflets.

The BCSS published the *Tarun Kranti*. Started by the Tarun Shanti Sena in April 1974, it became after June 5, the organ of the BCSS and TSS. The editor of the journal was a leader of the TSS, which was the publisher. The *Tarun Kranti* was published irregularly, four times a month. In content it had a Sarvodaya bias. Some local journals, modelled on the pattern of the *Tarun Kranti*, had also come out during the first six months of the movement; for example, S*angharsh* from Bhagalpur, *Chhatra* S*angharsh* from Muzaffarpur, and *Kranti Doot* from Chaibasa. Their circulation declined in 1975; their appearance became irregular, and some of them disappeared from the scene.

ISSUE-ORIENTED PROGRAMMES

The issue-oriented programmes can be divided into two categories as suggested by Jayaprakash himself,[34] (1) those which propagated the need for a struggle, involving confrontation with the authority ; and, (2) those which promoted constructive activities.

STRUGGLE PROGRAMMES

Several satyagrahas were launched as part of the struggle programme during the first year (1974-75), demanding the dissolution of the State Assembly. The longest of these was the satyagraha from June 7 to 12. Every day, a batch of satyagrahis, enrolled in advance by the BCSS and given a brief training in the Dos and Don'ts, sat at the gates of the State Assembly and the secretariat. They tried to prevent MLAs from attending the Assembly. On June 12, some of the volunteers assaulted and manhandled five legislators and tore their clothes while they were entering the Assembly gate. On coming to know of it, JP apologized to the Bihar Assembly for the incident. On the whole, however, such incidents were exceptions rather than the rule.

In all, 3407 persons participated in the satyagraha between June 7 and July 12 in Patna. A large number of them came from Patna, Bhagalpur, Santhal Parganas and Gaya, but some from other districts also.[35] An analysis of the satyagrahis reveals that nearly 6 per cent were children below the age of 15, and 75 per cent of them below 25, only 3 per cent being in their fitfties or sixties. Most of them were literate. It is difficult to give a caste-wise analysis because sizeable number of the respondents (45 per cent) refused to mention their castes. But it can be inferred from other characteristics that a large, if not an overwhelming, number of the participants belonged to the upper castes.[36]

In October and November the agitators gheraoed government offices to paralyse their working. On November 4, the ministers were gheraoed. The gherao programme often led to a confrontation between the police and the agitators, the latter waving black flags, throwing stones, putting up barricades on roads, and manhandling Congress leaders, and police resorting to bursting teargas shells, lathi-charges and firings.

Bandh was an attractive programme for youth. Bandhs were organized against repression or for paralysing the government. The Bihar bandh call between October 3 and 5 was the most important. It was considered to be the 'final and decisive' phase of the struggle for the dissolution of the State Assembly. Jayaprakash appealed to students, government employees, businessmen and workers to support the bandh. The Chamber of Commerce supported the call. But organized workers such as the All India Telegraph Engineering Employees' Union, Bihar Provincial Bank Employees' Association, Railway workers' Union, the Bihar State Committee of All India Trade Union Congress etc., opposed the bandh. Normal life all over the state, except in some industrial towns of south Bihar, remained paralysed on all the three days : all shops remained closed ; buses, rickshaws, cars etc., went off the roads ; law courts wore a deserted appearance ; government offices worked partially ; train services on many sections of the North-Eastern Railway were disrupted, the tracks at several places having been removed ; the telecommunication system was snapped and some stations were gheraoed by the supporters of the bandh. But it is worth noting that the examinees of B.A., B.Sc., I.Sc., etc., at different examination centres turned up as usual, and factories also kept working. Jayaprakash led the satyagraha at the secretariat gates on October 3 and 4. Confrontation between the Central Reserve Police (CRP) and the youth took place at several places; 13 persons, according to official sources, having been killed in police firing. About 2,500 persons were arrested. Dusk-to-dawn curfew was imposed on the second and third days of the bandh in six towns ; it was extended for one day in Patna and in a few other towns. Bihar returned normal only after October 7.

The "Dissolve Assembly Week" from on May 8, 1974 was observed by the BCSS and BJSS. Jayaprakash Narayan wrote an open letter to the MLAs asking them to resign in the interest of "good, clean and efficient government."[37] To the opposition MLAs (whose parties had supported the movement from the outset and many of whose leaders and members had courted arrest), he said : "So if you, opposition MLAs, continue to stick to your seats in the Assembly, you not only expose your erstwhile support as being hollow, but also become a party to all the wrongs perpetrated by the Bihar Government." The opposition parties also asked their MLAs to resign from the Assembly in support of the movement. A few opposition MLAs did, but a majority defied the directive. Later, some of them joined the Congress. Some studensts gheraoed the MLAs to force them to resign. In one such incident the security guards of the MLA opened fire injuring three persons.

No-Tax Campaign

In order to paralyse the government, JP asked the people in July not to pay taxes. But the programme did not receive any response in urban areas. In fact, it was claimed that commercial tax collection had increased by Rs. 18 crores in the first half of the year.[31] Several businessmen told me that they would donate money to the movement but at the same time pay taxes to the government. They wanted to avoid an open confrontation with the government for fear that it would confiscate their property if they failed to pay taxes. However, a few farmers did not pay the land revenue or the levy to the government .

Picketing of liquor shops was a part of the no-tax campaign, students taking a leading part in some towns. But the government and the liquor contractors joined forces, and the students were unable to resist the police and privately hired goondas of the shopkeepers. The picketing programme was therefore discontinued within a month. Similarly, the stir against cinemas was abandoned before it got off the ground. Gherao of government offices did not continue for many days either.

JANATA SARKAR

Jayaprakash Narayan called upon the people, soon after the three-day bandh in October 1974, to set up "people's assembly and parallel government" if the Assembly was not dissolved by a deadline "to be set in near feature". The CSSs and the JSSs were to set up candidates and hold elections to the people's assembly. The main tasks of the people's administration were to be : organization of Gram Shanti Dals for preventing crime and maintaining peace, distribution of essential commodities at fair price, building up of a proper atmosphere in the villages to ensure equal treatmeat to Harijans and prevent their eviction from homesteads, etc.

Soon after JP's announcement, reports of the formation of parallel government in three or four blocks were received. Some Sarvodaya workers hailed the news. One of them told me that this was the evidence of people's "strength and achievement". However, a reporter of the *Indian Nation*, who visited the Warsaliganj block in the of Nawada (claimed to be running a parallel government), reported :

> Supporters and active workers of JP led agitation in Nawada are more amused than jubilant over the reported claim of formation of a "parallel janata government" in the district... At Warsaliganj this reporter could not locate a single active worker of the Action Committee. Its office was also locked... Krishna Murari (16) is a student of class eleven in the school and he said he had heard of such

a government formed by JP. In answer to a question whether such an institution existed at Warsaliganj, he said : "Not here, but at Patna under JP's leadership."[39]

Annoyed by the report, workers of the Nawada CSS set fire to the parcels of the newspaper for two or three days. Later, JP put off the parallel government programme, saying it would be meaningless "without a robust organizational base".

In January 1975, JP gave the programme of Janata Sarkar, i.e. people's government. It was to be formed from the village upwards. The members of the village Janata Sarkar were to be elected unanimously by the entire adult population of the village, representatives from all the villages in the block would then elect their representatives for the block; the block representatives would in turn elect district representatives; and the members of district Janata Sarkars were to elect their state representatives. The Chhatra Sangharsh Samitis and Jana Sangharsh Samitis were to perform the executive functions of the Janata Sarkar. Each Janata Sarkars, at whatever level it was formed, would have a convenor, co-convener and a treasurer. The minimum programme for the Janata Sarkar was : adjudication of disputes, supervision of the distribution of essential commodities, distribution of bhoodan as well as government land, fighting against dowry system, verification of electoral rolls and campaigning for cleanliness. Needless to add, there is no significant difference between the programmes of the voluntary associations like youth organization and those of the Janata Sarkar. In fact, the term Sarkar is a mere appellation to catch the public eye.

It was decided to form Janata Sarkar in 150 blocks out of the 587 blocks in the state by the end of March 1975.[40] (Again in May 1975, a call was given to form Janata Sarkars in 300 blocks within three months.[41]) However, by the end of March 1975, only 18 blocks were declared to have formed Janata Sarkars. In early April 1975, I collected some data in respect of 8 Janata Sarkars. In many of the villages of these blocks CSS or JSS had not been formed. The members of the block level Janata Sarkar were not elected by any one. They were mostly, from the dominant sections of society and belonged to JSS or CSS. In Chandi block of Biharsharif district, for instance, the landed class had formed in January 1974 a Kisan Sangh to protect the interests of Kisans. The governing board of the Kisan Sangh converted itself into Jana Sangharsh Samiti, which was later converted into Janata Sarkar. It was dominated by the Jana Sangh and RSS workers. I found that 4 out of 8 Janata Sarkars had become inactive within two months of their formation. For example, the Janata Sarkar of Pakariwarawan block in Nawada district, which in January 1975 had arranged the sale of kerosene at a fixed price and also supervised the distribution of seeds and fertilisers was defunct in late March when I visited Pakariwarawan. There was no office, and the workers who were active in January, not knowing what else to do, turned to their personal affairs.

ELECTION

Jayaprakash Narayan and the Prime Minister, Mrs. Gandhi met on November 1, 1974 for ninety minutes. They discussed issues such as inflation, corruption, electoral reforms and educational reconstruction. The Prime Minister sought JP's co-operation in finding remedies for the various social and political ills. She said that they could not be successfully dealt with without public cooperation. But Mrs. Gandhi and JP could not reach a compromise over the issue of the dissolution of the Bihar Assembly. Mrs. Gandhi said that JP should wait till the next elections to know the will of the people. JP accepted this as a challenge, and added a new dimension of election to the struggle. He said, "Election will be part of the struggle. So the contest will be only between two parties— one of those who support the struggle and the other of those who oppose it. This will be a new type of election, part of the struggle." He appealed to people to work for the victory of 'their candidates' against Congress condidates. He said, "Whoever may be the candidate adopted or supported by the students' and people's committees, (you have to work for them), you have accepted the challenge. Now it will be for you to act."[42] JP's "revolutionary movement" was thus preparing itself for the forthcoming elections.

CONSTRUCTIVE PROGRAMMES

JP left for Vellore in April 1974 for a prostate operation. But he gave instructions to the CSSs and JSSs to continue their programme of ensuring sale of essential commodities at fixed prices. It may be recalled that in Patna, Muzaffarpur and in some other towns students had unearthed some hoarded goods. They had fixed the prices of some essential commodities and forced traders to sell at the prices so fixed. Flying squads were formed to keep a watch.[43] This led to a confrontation between the police and the hired goondas on one side and the volunteers on the other. JP said that "the fight against blackmarketing, profiteering, hoarding etc. will continue throughout the period" (of his absence). He gave a detailed programme :

> In Patna a Committtee has been set up by me to discuss the various aspects of the problem with the officials concerned. After that, meeting will be held with representatives of traders' associations, both wholesale and retail, as also with representatives of industries supplying some of the essential commodities, such as vegetable oil.

> Joint groups of officers and representatives of Chhatra and Jana Sangharsh Samitis will be formed to unearth ghost ration cards held by fair price shops. There will also be squads of volunteers of Chhatra and Jana Sangharsh Samitis to function as watchdogs to ensure that the agreed prices are adhered to and the scarce commodities alloted by the government to the shopkeepers do not disappear into the blackmarket. Should an occasion arise, peaceful forms of satyagraha will be launched in order to control prices and ensure the availability of commodities needed by the common people.[44]

It may be emphasized that JP's call to fight against hoarding, profiteering etc. was confined to unearthing ghost ration cards and negotiating with traders and government officials to fix the prices. A section of the boys took the programme seriously. But in general it did not make much headway. *The Indian Nation* reported, "Unscrupulous wholesalers and retail dealers are trying to defeat the commendable scheme— to end hoarding and profiteering. They are openly flouting the assurance they gave to the district magistrate to sell things at the mutually agreed rates. Essential commodities have either gone underground or are being sold at blackmarket rates."[45] The agitators tried to implement "the agreements" to sell the commodities at fixed prices. In such cases, the businessmen, their hired goondas and police beat up the boys. And the boys did not have any programme or organization to back their struggle. I was told by several workers of the CSSs that sons and relations of traders infiltrated the movement and sidetracked it. *The Times of India* reported, "There is some talk that hoarders and profiteers have been financing the students. Significantly, the godowns owned by profiteering wholesalers or shops belonging to retailers who raise prices without any provocation have not been picketed by students ?"[46]

Later, since JP characterized the economic programmes as 'constructive' rather than combative, he asked the volunteers to seek the co-operation of the government in dealing with blackmarketing and hoarding. But in September he held the government responsible for scarcity and high prices, and made it clear that the movement was not against any particular community.[47]

Another economic programme, viz., speedier implementation of land ceiling and bataidari laws, and distribution of legal documents for homestead land to Harijans, remained unimplemented. As for distribution of bhoodan and government land to landless labourers, it was unrealistic to expect young boys to accomplish in a short period what Bhoodan movement had failed to do in twenty years.

As part of the anti-corruption drive (which, according to JP was a 'constructive' programme), 'Sadachar Week' was observed between May 16 and 22, 1974. During this week sons and daughters of corrupt persons, including ministers, businessmen and big farmers, were expected to observe a twelve-hour fast in their homes to persuade their elders to end corrupt and anti-social practices. This programme was a flop. Students, Sarvodaya workers and party workers took a pledge during this week not to indulge in "corrupt practices". It should be noted that some students disclosed corrupt practices of officers. They also caught red-handed some officers taking bribes. But the volunteers not only failed to sustain their interest, but were unable to resist pressures, temptations and threats.

In response to Jayaprakash's appeal to visit villages and educate the voters, some students from different parts of the state visited villages in July and August 1974. But after a week or so they returned home and resumed their studies. They complained that they did not have any concrete programme for sustained work. Again in 1975, some students participated in flood relief work and vaccination programme against cholera.

The constructive programme did not overlook social reforms. To make a dent in the caste system, JP asked the high caste boys to give up the practice of wearing the sacred thread. This understandably caused some resentment among the orthodox Hindus, and so some volunteers, including Sarvodaya workers, found it necessary to explain it away by saying that JP had not asked people to discard the sacred thread for ever, but only till the Assembly was dissolved. Thus even a measure of social reform was given a political colour. Even when JP came to know of this explanation, he did not publicly clarify his position.

Another measure of social reform also failed to evoke a favourable response. This concerned dowry, a social practice, which, unlike the wearing of the sacred thread, could not claim to have a religious sanction. Even though JP pleaded that the taking and giving of dowry led to corruption, he failed to persuade many among his own youthful followers to turn their back on it.

ELECTORAL REFORMS

Critical as Jayaprakash Narayan was of the electoral system, he appointed an Electoral Reforms Committee to suggest changes in the electoral law. JP accepted the committee's report without any comment.

The committee claimed that its recommendations "are designed towards reducing the power of money and abuse of administrative machinery which distort the reflection of the popular will."[48]

On the issue of curbing money power, the committee made two observations :

(1) The steep rise in election expenses. particularly by the Congress Party which has access by reasons of its power of patronage to business finance, is the result of a deliberate preference in favour of money power as a major instrument for winning elections.

(2) The sums spent in general by candidates in elections till 1967 did not exceed by far the limits prescribed by law.

The above observations suggest that the committee was more concerned with the money power used by the Congress party. And their contention was that expenses incurred in elections had increased after 1967 or, say, since the 1971 elections. Contrary to these observations, newspaper reports and election studies reveal that even before 1967, all the political parties were spending much more than the stipulated ceiling. It would not be out of place to quote from a 'confidential' note, written by one of the members of the present committee, in 1961 to his party members. He said,

> I brought up the question of finance and mentioned that, since the General Secretary's constituency was endorsed by the party, Rs. 30,000 would be available from the party in addition to Rs. 25,000 which I would contribute from my personal resources, making a total of Rs. 55,000...He said that Rs. 55,000 would not be adequate for the constituency and I agreed to his suggestion that Rs. 75,000 or thereabouts should be made available, the balance to be from my own resources. Thus, a sum of Rs. 1,20,000 was to be allocated : Rs. 60,000 by the party and Rs. 60,000 from my own resources.[49]

The above note speaks for itself. Needless to add that the author of the above note was then the leader of the opposition party. The observations of the committee were not only biased but were designed to malign the Congress rather than to reform the electoral system.

Further, some of the important recommendations of the Committee were :

1. All recognised political parties should be required by law to keep full and accurate accounts, including their sources of income and details of expenditure. The accounts should be audited by Chartered Accountants

nominated by the Election Commission and should be open to public inspection on moderate charges. Keeping of false accounts should make the office-bearers of the party punishable as a cognizable offence.

2. In every constituency, all the amounts spent for the furtherance, directly or indirectly, of the prospects of a candidate in an election shall be disbursed through his election agent. These should include amounts spent by the candidate's political party or any organisation or persons supporting him. All contracts, whereby election expenses are incurred shall, in every case, be entered into by the candidate himself or by his agent and by nobody else.

3. The present limit of election expenses fixed for parliamentary and assembly elections should be doubled.

4. Deposits required from candidates should be increased from Rs. 500 to Rs. 2,000 in the case of parliamentary elections, and from Rs. 250 to Rs. 1,000 for election to an assembly or a council.

5. Any donation to a political party or for a political purpose upto Rs. 1,000 per year per assessee should be eligible for exemption under the Income-tax Act.

There is nothing new in the above mentioned recommendations. In one way or the other they were suggested earlier by different commissions. However, one wonders how these technically sound suggestions can curb the money power. Would the political parties maintain 'accurate' accounts ? And how far are 'accurate' accounts *correct* accounts ? What is important here is that the authors of the report ignore the subtle role of money power in Indian politics in general and elections in particular, and the fact that money is spent in various ways before and after elections which influence the election results.

It may also be noted that in as much as these recommendations would make elections even more costly than they are at present, they went against JP's main purpose to make elections cheap so that poor candidates could seek elections. The committee was silent about other major concerns of JP, viz., right to recall, decentralization of election system, etc. This is probably because these do not suit the philosophy and convenience of the opposition parties with which a majority of members of the committee sympathized.

EDUCATIONAL PROBLEMS

In order to bring about changes in the education system, JP held one or two seminars. He founded an institute known as 'Centre For New Education'. It aimed at bringing about an "alround radical transformation" in education. In April 1975, the centre was in its early stage. It was planning to organize certain 'training' programmes for youths. In an interview JP told me, "we have prepared an inventory of the students who have left college for the movement. We want to start classes to substitute their loss of studies. We are thinking of starting correspondence courses... We can also start courses for the students which can help them to get jobs". Such courses included typing, journalism, carpentary, etc. These courses are in no way new. JP himself was thus, going against his own philosophy of "delinking education from jobs". To my question : "How can such courses develop revolutionary spirit among the students", ? JP replied, "What else can be done ? Students have to earn. You cannot maintain them. It requires money". He added, "You cannot have a model of a revolution. Revolution develops in course of time. This is a new Revolution. There was never a peaceful revolution in history".

CADRE-BUILDING PROGRAMMES

Students were the vanguard of JP's Total Revolution. For, according to him, the proletariat ceased to be a revolutionary class; students, on the other hand, did not have any vested interest. He therefore, called upon students to give up their studies for one year for the cause of Total Revolution. Addressing them, he said, "Corruption, soaring prices and unemployment, are they not already corroding your lives ? Are they not already creating nightmarish conditions in your lives ? If you betray your fellow students, play false to those who are in jails or have given up their studies to devote themselves to the movement, the students and their movement will be suppressed by brute force, so that you won't be able to raise your heads for years to come"[50]. He argued that since the present education was meaningless for life, students would lose nothing in leaving colleges for a year. So as to reassure those who lost a year of college education, JP said, "Those who participate in the movement will naturally get some preference in government jobs" from their new government[51].

In June, JP appealed to students to boycott the examinations. Students were divided on the issue. Even those belonging to the ABVP (which was supporting the movement) were reluctant to follow him. *The Indian Nation* observed, "Our reading of the situation is that the students in general have high regard for Mr. Jayaprakash Narayan. They support the agitation but all of them are not prepared to sacrifice their careers for revolution in Bihar".[52] It may be noted that by calling for the boycott of examinations and for the closure of colleges, the BCSS, was reversing its earlier stand. It may be recalled that in March it had asked for the opening of the colleges; in July, it was threatening to launch a "guerilla satyagraha" to enforce closure for a year.[53] The CPI-dominated Bihar Chhatra Naujawan Sangharsh Morcha (BCNSM) opposed the move.

On the eve of reopening of colleges, the examination control room of Deoghar College was set ablaze. On July 13, the students of the CSS gheraoed the Kisan College at Biharsharif and compelled the students who were filling up admission and examination forms to leave. At Khagaria the Kashi College was locked up by the volunteers of the CSS. At places the CSS organized procession with the slogan "Pandraha July ke baad kya hoga, School-college bandh rahega". (School and colleges will remain closed after July 15.) Counter processions, supporting the reopening of colleges were organized by the BCNSM along with the non-CPI students who wanted to continue their studies. The students of Regional Institute of Technology, Adityapur, threatened to go on hunger strike if the authorities failed to reopen the college by July 1.

Clashes between groups favouring and opposing examination occurred as examinations began in July and August. At the Magadh University, Gaya, and some other places bombs were hurled. At Barh two groups exchanged fire. The government used all means to attract students to examinations. Attendance in the Intermediate examination differed from university to university. The Bhagalpur University registered the lowest number of examinees, the percentage being only 51.8; Mithila University attracted the largest number of students, 87.6 per cent[54]. After the examinations, several students, who had missed these demanded re-examination and an extension of the date of Public Service examinations.

Initially most students did not attend classes after the re-opening of colleges, but they registered their names and many paid their tuition fees. In September, about 10,000 students applied for admission to the first year of Arts, Science and Commerce classes in the various colleges of Patna University against the total number of 2,008 seats [55]. According to one survey, more than 90 per cent of students were inclined to join the colleges, working for the movement in their spare time.[56] Colleges remained closed whenever state-wide mobilizing programmes like procession, gherao or bandh were launched. The figures of students who left their colleges for one year was not available. Their number could not have been large.

The BCSS organized training camps for students to prepare cadre for the movement. At these camps Sarvodaya leaders gave speeches on several topics related to the Gandhian philosophy; discussions were also held on student movements elsewhere and in Bihar. Whatever may have been the impact of these camps on the trainees, it can be observed that some students started reading Gandhi and Jayaprakash. Nevertheless, they were sometimes baffled by what JP said to them, and did not always see any connection between his and their understanding of the various problems. Jayaprakash often scolded them for their indiscipline, corrupt practices and irresponsibility.

To sum up, the programmes were not in tune with the objectives of the movement. Most of them emphasized only one aspect of the movement: the dissolution of the State Assebly. Only political programmes found ready acceptance, the others relating to corruption and economic problems remaining non-starters. Students and youth—the vanguard of the movement—were mainly interested in the mobilizing programmes.

6. THE ACTORS

During the first year, the movement touched all parts of Bihar, but its intensity varied from place to place. It was at the lowest ebb in the industrial belt of south Bihar, most active in the cities and the countryside of Ganga-belt of north and south Bihar, particularly where the middle peasants have improved their economic condition since the 1960s.

Adivasis, Harijans and Muslims (about 36 per cent of the total population) had, by and large, remained indifferent to the movement, and so had poor peasants, landless labourers, industrial workers and casual labourers. However, during the early period, from March to May, the urban poor people were sympathetic to the movement because they felt that students were fighting for their cause. There were instances of rickshaw pullers not accepting the fare from students and, instead, asking the passenger, "Malik ! Chaval ek rupaya ser milega na ?" (Master ! will rice be available at one rupee a kilogram ?) But later, as issues like corruption and dissolution of the Assembly came to the fore, they grew cool because they saw the movement was not meant to solve the problems of the poor. No serious attempt was made to mobilize the working class. Indeed, some student leaders were opposed to the railway strike of May, 1974. On May 1, 1974 the BCSS observed the May Day, but the slogans that were raised by the procession taken out on that occasion demanded the dissolution of the Assembly. The next year, in 1975, May Day was not observed at all.

Similarly, the movement remained indifferent to poor peasants. In a rare instance a Sarvodaya worker mobilized about 150 poor peasants for a satyagraha at the block level. His colleagues did not appreciate this. And the attempt was never repeated.

The urban middle classes gave selective support, attending JP's meetings, observing bandhs and donating money to the movement, but stopping there—they had "to look after their business, their interests." Their sympathy with the movement notwithstanding, they forced their children to appear at examinations for the sake of their 'career'. However, businessmen who were in the beginning indifferent to the movement, as it was against price-rise, hoarding etc. joined it as it took a political turn.

The students and youth were the most active elements in the movement, but not in all programmes. Processions, demonstrations and bandhs attracted them in large numbers, but not so the picketing of liquor shops, visiting villages, and leaving colleges. In the course of the movement, they lost their credibility in the eyes of the masses. Several respondents, including Sarvodaya workers, reported to me that students were irresponsible and corrupt.

POLITICAL PARTIES

Political parties and their front organizations were in the forefront of the Bihar movement. The Jana Sangh, Congress (O), Socialist Party, Samyukta Socialist Party, and their front organizations, the ABVP, SYS, TSS and the Sarvodaya Mandal were the constituent partners of the movement.[56] Some other organizations, such as the RSS and Anand Marg supported or worked for the movement without wearing their particular labels. They received formal or informal instructions from their organizations as to the attitude they should adopt. They were identified by the other activists as the members of particular organizations.[57] Some parties such as the Communist Party of India (Marxist) (CPM) supported the movement but did not participate in it.

The CPM is a small party in Bihar. It had secured only 1.6 per cent of the total valid votes in the 1972 elections. The CPM supported the JP movement because it was opposed to the Congress party—the party of the monopoly bourgeoisie—capital but also because the movement had given voice to the important problems of the people. The party was particularly opposed to the repressive measures of the government. It called "on the people to protest against the brutal repression in Bihar and express their full solidarity with the fighting people of the state."[58] But it was critical of the several limitations of the movement, such as its failure to involve poor peasants, landless labourers and the working class, of its indifference to "the vital socio-economic problems of the toiling masses", and of its total dependence on students and the middle class which could not bring about a revolution. It was perturbed at the increasing hold of 'reactionary parties' like the Jana Sangh and the Anand Marg which "divert the mass discontent into wrong channels to serve their own selfish reactionary ends." The party kept aloof from the procession of June 5 and the gherao of November 4, although it supported the demand for the dissolution of the State Assembly.

The CPML, popularly known as the Naxalites, is an unorganized party. It advocates armed struggle in rural areas in order to annihilate the feudal forces. The Naxalites had organized landless labourers in some pockets, and created terror among the big landholders. The government came down heavily on them, arresting 1,422 alleged Naxalites between September 1969 and April 1971. The CPML supported the Bihar movement because it was against corruption, high prices, black-marketing, unemployment etc. and in the hope that it would change the system which protected vested interests. But its main reason was that the target of the movement was Mrs. Indira Gandhi who was 'authoritarian'[59]. However, the CPML was unhappy on two counts : one that the Congress (O) and the Jana Sangh were major partners; and two, that JP did not give radical economic programmes. So although they supported the movement, they did not actively participate in it.

The Socialist Party and Samyukta Socialist Party were actively involved in the movement, partly because of their anti-Congressism and partly because of their regard for Jayaprakash Narayan who was once their comrade-in-arms. Both the parties made all attempts to mobilize their supporters for the struggle, the students of the SYS went out to the countryside to draw in the peasants. But their organizations were in bad shape and as parties they were unable to recruit cadre for the movement. Within the movemen titself they found it difficult to make adjustments with the Jana Sangh workers. However, they had faith in JP and believed that he would give a radical socio-economic content to the movement and would oust the parties or groups which were not prepared to go along.

The Swatantra Party, now merged Bharatiya Lok Dal (BLD), the Congress (O) and the Jana Sangh, all accused the Congress of becoming 'authoritarian' and moving towards communism. They all oppose communism of any brand.

Of the three, the Jana Sangh was the most organized party working in the movement. Its members planned their strategies and followed them strictly. The JSS was strong in areas where the Jana Sangh was strong. The party co-ordinated its work with its two sister organizations, the ABVP and RSS.[60] The ABVP dominated the CSS at many places, and at some places RSS workers were either office-bearers of the CSS or guided the members of the CSS. RSS members worked as volunteers in processions and at JP's meetings. The ABVP, Jana Sangh and RSS, while working for the movement, maintained heir separate identities. The RSS ran its *shakhas* (centres) in jails, and ABVP maintained its office as centre of activities, and made attempts to recruit boys from the movement. The Jana Sangh and ABVP workers felt that through the movement they had put the CPI at least five years behind. They did not agree with all that JP said. One of them told me that if after the dissolution of the Assembly JP gave some economic programme they would oppose him. They thought that apart from the fact that the Congress would be defeated in the election held after the dissolution of the Assembly, there would be no change in the situation. A prominent state level leader of the ABVP said to me, "I do not think that some big changes will take place after the dissolution. JP will be busy with his Sarvodaya work and we will be busy with Vidyarthi Parishad."

Anand Marg has many followers in Bihar, mainly from among doctors, civil servants including IAS officers, and engineers etc. It had not come into the movement as an organization, but it allowed its members (for the sake of "moral revolution") to support the movement to see the Congress defeated, and to participate in dharnas and processions. One Anand Marg Avadhoot[61] told me, "We Avadhoots in dress do not participate in the agitation. Our civilian Margis participate. If they are caught, how can they be identified as Anand Margis?" However, their participation was only marginal, and they had no faith in JP.

Sarvodaya workers who were engaged in various constructive activities such as bhoodan, khadi, relief work, village reconstruction etc. were very active in the movement.[62] They regarded the movement as their own. Their intimate connection is given separate treatment in the next chapter.

Opposed to the movement were the Congress and the CPI. The Congress saw the movement as aimed at itself. The Congress government did take certain measures to check prices; a fow hoarders were arrested, the quantum of ration supplied to hostel in mates was raised ; a few officers were suspended or dismised on charges of corruption. But there was no sustained follow-up action and these measures were half-hearted. The Congress government dealt with the Bihar movement merely as a law and order problem. The party which professed the principle of prohibition used force against those who were picketing liquor shops. The government depended upon the Central Reserved Police, State Reserved Police and the army to suppress the movement; several hundred youth and political leaders were put behind the bars under the Maintenance of Internal Security Act (MISA); universities were turned into government departments, a few teachers being suspended for participating in the movement.

The Congress Party left it to its youth wings the Youth Congress to organize a few processions, some public meetings and seminars or conferences as a counter-offensive. But the Congress leaders had lost confidence in themselves and shied away from facing their constituents. They moved around with the help of hired goondas and police, and used money to buy over youth leaders. All they did was to brand the movement as "fascist" or "counter-revolutionary".

The CPI believes that the Congress is controlled by the national bourgeoisie, and that the monopoly bourgeoisie which is outside the Congress, is creating a situation in which fascists can come to power. After 1973 the CPI supported the Congress to fight "imperialist and monopoly capitalists". Since it felt that the JP movement was also against communism, it opposed the movement tooth and nail, denouncing it as a reactionary movement. The party organized some processions of the poor peasants, working class and white collar employees against the movement, and held domonstrations against high pirces, blackmarketing, hoarding etc. at block and district head-quarters. It also published several leaflets and booklets opposing the movement.

Thus, the non-CPI communist parties who cherish the idea

of bringing about a revolution, though supported the movement, remained outside it. The SSP and Sarvodaya workers opted for revolution, but the former was unorganized and worked around personalities, while the latter, as we shall see in the next chapter, were confused in their philosophy, vacillating from status quo to revolution. And ironically, the parties and groups, which really opposed revolution, dominated the 'revolutionary movement'.

7. AN OVERVIEW

After 18th March 1974, Jayaprakash Narayan canalized sporadic riots and agitation into an organized, planned and 'peaceful' movement. He provided it a philosophical base, a goal and a direction. The upsurge over economic grievances—often against businessmen—was given a political content, and the Congress government was made the target of attack as the fountain-head of rampant corruption, high prices, blackmarketing, mis-education, electoral malpractices, etc. If the participants of the movement were of one mind with regard to dislodging the Congress from power, it did not mean that they were all agreed as to the causes that bred corruption and economic hardships. Many were sceptical of JP's concepts and philosophy, especially his "Total Revolution". Even those who did believe in revolution doubted if it could be brought about through the present movement.

Between the issues that were taken up from time to time and the professed objective of the movement there was often no perceptible connection. Not all the programmes, lopsided as they were, were well received by the followers. Some programmes were announced for their publicity value, and there they remained ; some did not get off the ground ; and some fizzled out soon after they were launched ; only mobilizing programmes of processions, demonstrations and meetings demanding the dissolution of the Assembly were taken up enthusiastically by the leading elements of the movement.

The movement was not broad-based ; it was confined to certain areas of the state and certain sections of society. The urban middle class and students who were active in the pre-March 1974 agitations continued to remain active in the movement. Two groups entered the movement after 18 March businessmen and rich and neo-rich farmers. Businessmen were against the agitation in February and March because students were engaged in bringing down prices and unearthing hoarded stocks. They started supporting the movement when it took a political turn. The farmers had already been agitating against the government, demanding more agricultural facilities and higher prices for their products ; they were thus predisposed to make common cause with the movement directed against the government. Industrial workers, who had joined hands with the middle class in January 1974, kept aloof from the movement. The movement failed to draw in poor peasants, agricultural labourers and casual labourers.

The non-communist political parties and Sarvodaya organizations became, officially or unofficially, the constituent partners of the movement ; the Jana Sangh and its student wing, the ABVP, came to occupy a dominant position in the movement, with the Sarvodaya workers trying to check them.

NOTES

1. *Everyman's*, June 22, 1974.
2. Ajit Bhattacharjea, *Jayaprakash Narayan : A Political Biography*, Delhi, Vikas Publishing House, 1975.
3. Ibid.
4. Quoted by Vasant Nargolkar, *JP's Crusade for Revolution*, New Delhi, S. Chand & Co. (Pvt.) Ltd., 1975.
5. Ibid.
6. Quoted ibid.
7. Minoo Masani, Jayaprakash Narayan, *Encounter*, December 1975.
8. Geoffrey Ostergaad, Prelude to the Bihar Movement : Sarvodaya And the Search for Non-violent Revolution in India. (mimiographed) Birmingham. Department of Politics, TheUniversity of Birmingham,1976.
9. *Everyman's*, December 29, 1973.
10. Laxminarayan Lal, *Jayaprakash* (Hindi) Delhi, Macmillan, 1974.
11. *Everyman's* December 22, 1973.
12. Ibid , February 23, 1974.
13. Technically, the purse was given by the Reception Committee of the people of Bardoli taluka. But the committee was dominated by rich peasants, belonging to the Khedut Samaj.
14. *Everyman's*, July 20, 1974.
15. Ibid., December 22, 1974.

16. Ibid., December 1, 1974.
17. Ibid., July 20, 1974.
18. J.P. Narayan, Education Plan For Students In Stir, *The Indian Nation*. September 5, 1974.
19. *Everyman's*, December 1, 1974
20. N.S. Jagannathan, A Revolution in the Making, *The Hindustan Times*. August 26, 1974.
21. *Everyman's*, June 1, 1974.
22. *Tarun Kranti* (Hindi), October 2, 1974.
23. *Everyman's*, November 23, 1974.
24. Ibid., December 8, 1974.
25. Ibid., December 1, 1974.
26. *The Indian Express*, May 23, 1974.
27. *Everyman's*, June 22, 1974.
28. Ibid.
29. Ibid., June 22, 1974.
30. Ibid., June 15, 1974.
31. Ibid.
32. Ibid, November 23, 1974.
33. For the list of slogans see *Tarun Kranti*, June 2, and November 1, 1974.
34. *Everyman's*, August 17, 1974.
35. *Tarun Kranti*, July 3, 1974.
36. Partha N. Mukherji, Who are JP's followers, *Everyman's*, November 1974. A similar analysis of 400 satyagrahis of Saran district was made by Nageshwar Prasad. See, Profile of the men and women behind the Bihar movement, *Everyman's*, February 16, 1975. However, Nageshwar Prasad's analysis is oversimplified. He analysed certain variables in which as many as 67.5 per cent cases were not ascertained. The analysis of land-ownership and income appears to be misleading. Most of the satyagrahis were students, and as students they often don't mention, except when specifically asked, the land owned by their parents. I shall only mention here that there is only 20 per cent literacy in Bihar, and that most of the landless are illiterate. Thus, an educated but landless agricultural labourer is rare.
37. *Everyman's*, May 18, 1974.
38. *The Economic Times*, December 10, 1974.
39. Ibid. October 16, 1974.
40. O.P. Deepak, Is Jana Sarkar Some Sort of a Parallel Government ? *Everyman's*, February 2. 1975.
41. *The Indian Nation*, May 23, 1975.
42. *Everyman's* November 23, 1974.
43. *Muzaffarpur me Gandhi Shanti Pratisthan Aur Tarun Shanti Sena ki Bhumika*, Patna, Bihar Sarvodaya Mandal, 1974.
44. *Everyman,s*, April 27, 1974.
45. Ibid., May 29, 1974.

46. *The Times of India*, (New Delhi), May 7, 1974.
47. *Tarun Kranti*, October 2, 1974.
48. *The Indian Express*, February 25, 1975.
49. A copy of the letter is in the author's file.
50. Ibid., July 20, 1974.
51. Ibid.
52. Ibid., July 1, 1974.
53. *The Times af India*, (Ahmedabad) July 15, 1974.
54. *The Indian Nation*, September 19, 1974.
55. Ibid., September 6, 1974.
56. *The Indian Express*, (Bombay), December 2, 1974.
57. However JP asserts, "I have repeatedly denied publicly that the Anand Marg had or has *anything to do* with the Bihar movement. To my knowledge, there is no Anand Margi in any of the Sangharsh Samitis or is the Anand Marg a constituent body of the State, District, Block or lower Sangharsh Samitis...As for the RSS, it too is not formally a part of the movement, though I dare say there are many members of the organization participating in it. But I shall still point out that the RSS, as an organization, is not a constituent part of the movement in Bihar or elsewhere". (emphasis added), Jayaprakash Narayan replies, *The Illustrated Weekly*. April 27, 1978. Technically speaking JP is correct.
58. *People's Democracy*, June 30, October 13, and November 10, 1974.
59. *Sankalap*, (Hindi) Farukhabad, September 28, 1974.
60. The workers of the RSS and ABVP assert strongly that they are not front organizations arguing that the Jana Sangh was born later than both. This is true, but the RSS and ABVP provide cadre to the Jana Sangh. The volunteers of these organizations work for the Jana Sangh in elections, demonstrations and seminars. See Craig Baxter, *Jana Sangh : A Biography of an Indian Political Party*. Philadelphia, University of Pennsylvania Press. 1969.
61. An Avadhoot is one who dedicates his life to establish *Sadvipra* society, the society of the Anand Marg conception. The Avadhoots put on saffron coloured uniform of the Marg.
62. However, the Sarva Seva Sangh as an ogranization did not participate in the movement. It left its members free to decide whether to participate or not. Thus, technically, Sarvodaya Mandal was not a constituent partner.

4

Sarvodaya and the Bihar Movement

We have noted earlier that Jayaprakash Narayan, the leader of the Bihar movement, and his other Sarvodaya colleagues tried their best to keep the movement within the Sarvodaya framework : Gandhian ethics and economics were taught in the training camps and literature on Gandhi and Jayaprakash was widely distributed. In this chapter we shall examine the Sarvodaya ideology and the working of the Sarvodaya movement during the last two decades. We shall also try to find out why the majorty of the Sarvodaya workers decided to support the Bihar movement.

It should be noted at the outset that Sarvodaya workers, coming mainly from the middle classes, are sensitive to human suffering, but also somewhat utopian in their ideas. It appears that they were suffering from a sense of frustration during the 1970s. They were upset over the increasing poverty and growing violence in the country, but also felt disappointed with the performance of the Sarvodaya movement itself. Before we examine what role these objective and subjective factors played in drawing the Sarvodaya workers toward the Bihar movement, we shall briefly dwell on Sarvodaya philosophy.

1. SARVODAYA PHILOSOPHY

The Sarvodaya movement, working under the auspices of the Sarva Seva Sangh, is an off-shoot of the Gandhian movement of the pre-independence era. Mahatma Gandhi combined social reform activities—or constructive activities, as he called them—and politics. He raised a band of dedicated constructive workers, who, though not actively involved in day-to-day political activities, were part of and participated in the freedom movement. The political arm of the freedom movement, the Indian National Congress, emphasized, in theory if not in practice, constructive work as essential for Congressmen. However, after independence, constructive and political work came to be tackled at two different organizational levels. Gandhi wanted the Congress to dissolve itself and convert itself into the Lok Sevak Sangh. The Congress leaders did not heed his advice. And the Congress has since remained a political party. The constructive workers formed, after Gandhi's assassination, the Lok Sevak Sangh, later named Sarva Seva Sangh—the association for the service of all. It is an umbrella organisation of all fields of constructive activities started during Gandhi's lifetime.

The basic principle of the Sangh is *sadhan-suddhi*, that is, purity of means. Sarvodaya philosophy equates right means with non-violent means. At the first conference of constructive workers, Vinoba Bhave observed : "We may hold different views on other matters; but if we could agree on this basic principle, many of our difficulties shall vanish. If we could forge a united front on this foundation (non-violence), it shall be a great achievement, indeed"[1].

Sarvodayaists strive towards in a society based on truth and non-violence, in which there will be no distinction of caste or creed; no opportunity for exploitation, and full scope for the development of both individuals and groups. 'Truth' in its non-metaphysicle aspect means personal morality : man should be good, selfless and honest. It should be noted, however, that what is 'good' and 'honest' is not clearly defined.

In order to attain its goal, the Sarva Seva Sangh suggests several constructive programmes including Bhoodan, Gramswaraj, communal unity, development of khadi and other village industries, removal of narrow provincialism, cow protection, naturopathy etc. The Sangh is, "not a political or a religious body. Nor it is wedded to any particular 'ism'. Any person who agrees with its aims and earnestly believes in Truth and Non-violence *as the only correct conduct* can deem himself as a *Sevak* of the Samaj (Sangh), whatever political, economic and religious opinions he might hold. Nobody can object to his claim to be such a Sevak"[2]. (emphasis added)

Thus non-violence is sacrosant to Sarvodaya philosophy.

PARLIAMENTARY DEMOCRACY

One of the basic concepts of Sarvodaya is Gram Swaraj which envisages decentralization of economy and political power to preserve and develop the freedom of the people. Vinoba Bhave says, "There will be no freedom until every village and community controls its own life, runs its own affairs, settles its own quarrels, decides how its children shall be educated, undertakes its own defence, and manages its own markets. Only when power is decentralized and is in the hands of communities can there be a general renewal of self-confidence, and ordinary people everywhere can get some experience of social organization"[3].

Sarvodaya considers government unnecessary, and when it is centralized, an evil. If there must be a government, its activities should be minimal : "The best kind of government is one where it is possible to doubt whether any government exists at all. ...An ideal government would have no armaments, no police force and no penalties; the people would manage their own affairs, listen readily to advice, and allow themselves to be guided by moral considerations"[4].

Sarvodaya shuns power politics because, in its view, *rajniti*, i.e. power politics, is destructive of social development in that it creates conflicts and disturbs social harmony. In *rajniti*, individuals or political parties serve their own interests at the cost of the interests of all. Sarvodaya considers parliamentary democracy based on party system a sham because people do not have a say in the working of the government. "The whole arrangement", Vinoba believes, "in fact is bogus. Not only does it fail to express the people's strength, it also does even more harm than our former kings could do because our government can now claim to 'represent public opinion'."[5]

In regard to the relationship between Sarvodaya workers and politics, Vinoba Bhave and Jayaprakash Narayan, however, differ Vinoba believes that the Sarvodaya workers should shun all contact with politics. He argues that "the desire to keep contact with something, even in order to destroy it, is a subtle and insidious illusion."[6] Jayaprakash, on the other hand, holds the view that they should take interest in politics, though not, of course, in party politics. In his presidential address to the 13th All India Sarvodaya Sammelan (conference), in 1961, he explained, "It means, of course, that we do not belong to any political party, that we do not and shall not take part, directly or indirectly, in any political contest for position or power. But does it also mean that we are not concerned with what is happening in the political field ? With the working of our democracy and its various institutions ? If democracy were to be in peril, if there was a danger of political chaos, of dictatorship, shall we sit back smugly and twiddle our thumbs on the ground that we have nothing to do with politics ? Perhaps it is not understood clearly that our policy not to be involved in party and power politics is meant precisely to enable us to play a more effective and constructive part in moulding the politics of the country"[7].

Judged by the participation of Sarvodaya workers in elections, their aloofness from parliamentary democracy has increased. Thirty-three per cent of the Sarvodaya workers did not exercise their franchise in the 1952 elections, and their number doubled (66 per cent) in 1962 elections[8]. Figures for the subsequent elections are not available, but it is a safe guess that the number increased further.

The Sarvodaya advocates *lokniti*, i.e. people's politics, in which people have a direct say in the decisions which concern them, their community and the nation. *Lokniti* can develop into people's democracy in which gram sabha or ward sabha is the basic unit of the political structure. In such a decentralized political system, as Gandhi envisaged, the people of the village elect their delegates for the council at the district level, and the members of the district council elect the members of the state assembly. For its successful functioning Jayaprakash Narayan emphasized unanimity or consensus in decision making at all levels. He says, "All the decisions of the gram sabha or its executive should be either unanimous, by general consensus or *nem con*...The second requirement is that no one residing in the village or the urban or the work community who belongs to a political party should be elected by the gram sabha or the other primary democracies to any office"[9].

The founding fathers of the Constitution, however, did not

pay much attention to Gandhian concepts of political and economic structure. The formation of village panchayats as the operationalization of the concept of decentralization was paid lip sympathy and put in one article in the Directive Principles as an after-thought.[10] The Constitution, following the British model, adopted a parliamentary system of government in which political parties are imperative. This is in contradiction with the principles of Sarvodaya philosophy.

During the last twenty-five years, despite the formation of panchayati raj in some states, political authority has remained concentrated at the Centre. The Sarvodaya leaders feel that people do not have any say in the present form of government. Jayaprakash observes, "The people, by and large, are fed up with all political parties and the present form and practice of democracy. They go alongwith it and willy-nilly play their part, which is a nominal one in any case, namely, that of casting their vote once in a while, because there is no alternative before them."[11] And yet, people's faith in the miraculous powers of politics" has increased ; they have become increasingly dependent on government, and most decisions in a village or a state are taken with political considerations.

Owing to government sponsored welfare programmes, people have lost the initiative of villagers for their own development. Vinoba says: "Today, in the name of the 'Welfare State', we are concentrating all powers in the centre. Even if people do get a certain amount of benefit out of it, I would still call it not 'well' fare, but 'ill' fare, because it keeps power in the hands of a few. The idea of democracy will spread only when power is shared out among the people."[12]

PLANNING

Contrary to Gandhian principles, the Five Year Plans gave more importance to big industries rather than to cottage industries and agriculture. Vinoba argued with the government : "You have set up ginning presses and stopped hand-ginning and carding which was prevalent in millions of cottages. The Ministers are always willing to inaugurate factories, but never care to encourage village industries. There were many indigenous oil *ghanis* (*i.e.*, oil expellers) in various parts of the country to provide productive employment to the people. Now the goverement has allowed the installation of oil-expellers, and the *ghanis* have to be closed down. This is mechanical not a natural process ; the Government is directly responsible for smothering rural industries through its present pattern of planning".[13]

Again, the government gave priority to the family planning programme. Vinoba's reaction was : "Family planning is a question of altering the basic values of life. Artificial methods may control births, but do not change the mode of living. On the contrary, they erode moral values. If the Planning Commission cares a trifle for these values, I have nothing to say... In my view, it is not the weight of numbers but of sin that is [the] real burden on earth."[14] Thus, Sarvodaya opposed the basic political structure and planning in post-independence India.

CLASS COLLABORATION

Development of all is another cardinal principle of Sarvodaya philosophy. The apparent conflict of interests between various sections of society, according to this view, are artificial and illusory. Vinoba argues, "Sarvodaya means that the good of all resides in the good of one. That there could be interests of one person, which are against the interest of another, is inconceivable similarly, there could be no interests of any one community, class or country which would be against the interests of any other community, class or country. The idea of opposition of interests is itself wrong.".[15] Sarvodaya, therefore, emphasizes class collaboration. Empirical evidence, however, points to an accentuation of the class conflict,[16] even in the areas where the Sarvodaya workers have done intensive work.

Sarvodaya philosophy opposes capitalist economic system which brings in its train centralization and profiteering, although some of the cardinal principles of capitalism, such as individual freedom, minimum interference of the government in social and economic fields are part of the Sarvodaya philosophy. Industrialization, it believes, leads to dehumanization of society, but it thinks that capitalism has "lost all vitality."[17] In place of capitalism Sarvodaya advocates trusteeship, in which owners of factories and farms act as trustees of the property and work in the interest of all. Nevertheless, some concession has been given to personal property in the Bhoodan movement itself. And Sarvodaya leaders ignore 'capitalist' development in the country.

SARVODAYA AND COMMUNISM

Sarvodaya is opposed to communism. Apart from their common profession of belief in an egalitarian society, they differ in everything else—in their concept of egalitarian society, in their means of bringing it about, and in their assessment of the present society. Communists believe in the hegemony of the working class to build a new social order. They feel that reforming the condition of the have-nots would not lead to an egalitarian society. Such a society can be ushered in only through class struggle and not through a dialogue between the capitalists and the proletariat. Such class struggle could result in change of ownership of means of production, from individual to society. In order to develop the struggle, communists believe in developing class consciousness among working class. Sarvodaya, on the other hand, believes that harmony between the classes is good and conducive for all, and for a better social order, and therefore eschews class conflict. Sarvodaya workers are asked to dedicate themselves "to the *service* of the poor with single-minded devotion." It is the duty of the rich to *serve* the poor. Thus they have benevolent attitude towards the poor.

While communism advocates a change of economic structure and material condition, Sarvodaya pleads for development of moral character. Vinoba says, "the social structure changes its form along with the development of human character. Hence, all lovers of good should concentrate their attention on the development of moral qualities."[18]

According to Sarvodaya, communism is an evil, therefore it should be prevented. Vinoba believes, "If we do not carry on our work properly, communism is bound to make inroads into our public life". The differences between communism and Sarvodaya, according to Bhave, are "fundamental", and "irreconcilable". Vinoba believes that, "ultimately it will be Gandhism with which communism will have its trial of strength"[19].

The ideology of communism developed in Europe. It believes in internationalism. It does not believe in supernatural power. Sarvodaya considers communism as a 'foreign' ideology. Sarvodaya draws inspiration and draws its sustenance from the religious epics written several centuries ago. It is based on the traditional ethos of Indian community.

Many Sarvodaya workers were therefore disturbed that during the sixties, the communist parties emerged as strong parties in some states of north, south, and east India. Even in Bihar, where the Sarvodaya workers have worked intensively, the influence of communists has increased, the extremists among them known as Naxalites, having penetrated rural areas. They apprehended that the communists had infiltrated into the Congress party and the ruling party was tending to depend more on the Communist Party of India.

Thus, the basic philosophy of Sarvodaya is a mixture of anarchism and laissez faire of the nineteenth century which believed in the good of all through the good of individuals and with the minimum interference of government. Sarvodaya workers ignores the contradictions in their philosophy. They accept some important principles of capitalism but reject the consequences that flow from the capitalist system i.e. concentration of wealth and power in a few hands.

2. PERFORMANCE

In this section we shall deal with the internal situation in the Sarvodaya movement itself. The main constructive activities of the Sarvodaya movement are : Bhoodan, i.e. sharing o f land, and Gramdan, i.e. common ownership of village land. Rich farmers are expected to donate land voluntarily to be distributed among the landless families of the village. This is considered an alternative to the communist method of seizing land by force. (It may be recalled that Bhoodan was born in Andhra in 1951 following the communist uprising in Telangana.) It depends for its success on a change of heart of rich people. Vinoba says, "I believe that hearts do change, and non-violence alone is the remedy for all our ills... A psychological revolution like this cannot be brought about by violence. It can be ushered in only through the methods of Buddha, Christ and Gandhi".[20]

The Bhoodan movement roused some enthusiasm among the people. By 1957 the Bhoodan movement had been donated 4.2 million acres of land for redistribution. Vinoba then launched the Gramdan movement, which called not for donations of a proportion of every landowner's land, but for the complete surrender of property rights in land in favour of the village community. Explaining the basic idea of Gramdan, Vinoba said, "In the world today there are in fact no 'have-nots', some possess land, others property, and yet others intellect and physical labour. Furthermore, love and affection permeate the hearts of all human beings. In Gramdan the landlords should donate land and the working class their labour for the development of the community".[21] According to the scheme, one-tenth of the land in the Gramdan village was to be reserved for cultivation on a co-operative basis and the rest allowed to be used by the agriculturists during their lifetime. However, as the idea of Gramdan did not evoke the expected response, Vinoba evolved a simpler form of it and called it *Sulabh gramdan*. Under *Sulabh gramdan*, 75 per cent of the cultivators in a village were to contribute at least 5 per cent of their land for redistribution among the landless, retaining 95 per cent for their own cultivation with the legal ownership transferred to the village community. It made a distinction between 'ownership' and 'possession', that is, a person joining gramdan might surrender ownership of his entire land in a village without giving up possession of the entire area. The idea of Block-dan, District-dan and State-dan were later evolutions of Gramdan

Vinoba and other Sarvodaya workers toured almost the whole of the country on foot. State governments passed legislations to legalize the donation and the distribution of land, and the co-operative departments paid special attention to gramdan villages. By October 1969, the movement had received 4,176,815 acres of land in Bhoodan, 140,020 villages in Gramdan, 1030 blocks in Block-dan and 30 districts in District-dan. Vinoba spent 27 months in Bihar during the early fifties and again about four years in the late sixties in the cause of State-dan. Jayaprakash Narayan also concentrated his energies in Bihar since 1954, and more than one thousand Lok Sevaks worked for the mission. By the end of the Gandhi Centenary Year, 1969, the movement received dan, i.e. gift, of 98 per cent of the 587 blocks in Bihar, which may be regarded as Bihar-dan.

The figures are indeed impressive, but, like the government, the Bhoodan and Gramdan movements achieved their targets only on paper. The Gramdan villages, before Sulabha gramdan, were generally small, very poor and concentrated in low-caste and tribal areas. The movement is confined to a few states; about 50 per cent of the total donated land in the country is located in Bihar, and 80 per cent of the total Bhoodan land is concentrated in four states, viz. Bihar, Rajasthan, Uttar Pradesh and Madhya Pradesh. Roughly one-half of the land received in Bhoodan is uncultivable. Change of heart does not seem to have played any important role in the donation of land. According to one survey, "only 16 per cent land was donated (by 33 per cent donors) on ideological considerations and under charismatic influence. In about 30 per cent cases (involving 27 per cent land) the donations were made under moral and social pressures. About 13 per cent donors donated about 18 per cent land with a view to deriving some material gain in future. Finally it may be noted that in 15 per cent cases the Bhoodan-holders were relatives or servants or tenants of the donors".[22]

Despite all efforts of the Sarvodaya workers, equitable distribution of land in Bihar was still a far cry, and the power structure in rural society remained unchanged. Actually, the position of the landed class has become stronger during the last two decades. For its gifts of a small portion of land and for its hypocritical acceptance of Bhoodan at the normative level, the landed class has acquired respectability and the approbation of Sarvodaya workers. And any resistence on the part of the have-nots against the exploiters had been condemned or pacified by Sarvodaya workers on moral grounds of non-violence and common interests. On the continuing tensions in rural society, Pradhan H. Prasad in his study on Musahari block observes, "The power balance remains tilted against the vast mass of the people... the overlords have strengthened themeselves economically and politically on account of this movement". He concludes, "The approach of conversion by 'gentle persuasion' and of 'resolution of conflicts and problems by mutual adjustment leading to a juster and better social order' has failed".[23]

It may be that while people accept the idea of Bhoodan at the normative level, the donors, when required to actually transfer land, hesitate. Jayaprakash Narayan himself admits that Gram Swarajya or Nagar Swarajya has not worked well. "In block after block (people) signed papers (stating) that they would give up a share of their land. But when we went back to them to get the land, they began to make a lot of excuses... Saharsa district was taken up for intensive development to be a model for the whole country. A lot of effort went into this, but apart from five or six blocks it was a failure".[24] In some cases the donors have forcibly taken back their land after it was distributed. Hence, some Sarvodaya workers were losing interest in the movement and some had 'quietly dropped out of the movement altogether'. Geoffrey Ostergaad observes, "Vinoba himself by 1972 appeared to be losing interest in Gramdan or, at least, reconciling himself to the fact that nothing spectacular could be expected from it in the foreseeable future. In his speeches he began to dwell more on his other concerns, particularly the need to synthesize scientific and spiritual knowledge, and also to suggest other programmes".[25]

Some Sarvodaya leaders started doubting the effectiveness of persuasion and the change-of-heart approach. They felt that to "conversion by gentle persuastion" should be added non-violent, non-cooperation or resistance. According to a survey in 1965, the average Sarvodaya activist was not altogether convinced by Vinoba's concept of 'positive' satyagraha with its 'gentle, gentler, gentlest' approach.[26] He felt that 'negative' satyagraha will be necessary at some stage if not 'immediately'. During the early seventies, a section of the Sarvodaya workers openly advocated the need for non-violent agitation to break 'caste and political forces'.[27] Some of them organized satyagrahas in a few villages of Tamilnadu for distribution of land. Significantly, the Sarva Seva Sangh supported in July 1973 the statewide agitation for prohibition in Rajasthan.

For all their views of the role of government, Sarvodaya

workers found themselves increasingly dependent on the government. They could not keep out the government even from their own programmes. For instance, after receiving a village in Sulabh Gramdan, the Sarvodaya workers used to leave for another village (they too had targets to achieve), leaving development work to the community development departments. In fact, more often than not they have become mere agents of welfare programmes of the government. Many Bhoodan workers get their salaries out of government funds that the Bhoodan Yagna Committee receives. The same is the case as regards Khadi workers or the employees of relief work. Hence, their programmes have largely become government programmes and they are left with the task of implementing them as government employees.[28] They feel that they have very little scope to use their initiative. In his study on Vedchhi movement, I.P. Desai observes:

> All those developments in components of the movement indicate the stablization and routinization of the activities which rob the movement of its elan and original character... The activities continue but the movement seems to be dying. There is at least a lurking awarensss among the workers of what is happening. Though there is no clear diagnosis, the thinking centres around their relation with the government. As it appears there is no other source of finance. If therefore, they have to depend on the government, the government must be at least sympathetic to them and they must be sympathetic to it. But this cannot be assured. Should they therefore participate in the political process or not? There is no unanimity on the answers to this question. 29

Towards the end of sixties, enthusiasm for building 'Sarvodaya Samaj' was at its lowest ebb among the Sarvodaya workers. Many, if not all of them were becoming "dull and spiritless" and bogged down in "petty quarrels"[30] Ironically enough, 'corruption' also crept in even among the Sarvodaya workers themselves[31]. A prominent pro-JP Sarvodaya leader said in anguish, "The Congress has finished Gandhi's non-violence, and the constructive programme has finished Gandhi's truth."[32]

3. SARVODAYA AND THE CONGRESS PARTY

The Congress and the Sarva Seva Sangh, as noted above, are off-shoots of the same independence movement. The post-independence relationship between the two has been one of love and hate. Sarvodaya leaders have occasionally criticized the policies of the Congress, but they never confronted and challenged the party till the Bihar movement.

The inherent differences between the two—one had inherited state power and proposed to wield it, and the other looked askance at it—were sought to be papered over in the initial stages of independence. It may be recalled that soon after Gandhi's assassination a conference of political and constructive workers was organized in Sevagram from 11 to 14 March, 1948. It was attended, among others, by Jawaharlal Nehru, Rajendra Prasad, Maulana Abul Kalam Azad, Acharya Kripalani, Vinoba, Shankarrao Deo, Kishorlal Mashruwala, Jayaprakash Narayan and R. R. Diwakar. Nehru who, as Prime Minister, was trying to grapple with the country's, problems of great magnitude and complexity, addressed the conference thus : "Khadi is always important. But the basic problem is to arrest the wave of violence and prevent further disintegration of the country. We have to protect and safeguard the very freedom and integrity of India. In this larger context, talk of mere constructive work becomes rather artificial and unreal". He asserted that the Congress had to work ceaselessly for the social and economic freedom of India, and sought the co-opration of constructive workers in the task of building a new nation: "The Congress must maintain its close link with various constructive organizations".[33] Vinoba responded: "Panditji's difficulties are real, I fully sympathise with him. But he who wears the crown can alone suggest a way out. We have all to work together and share each other's worries and problems. Panditji's difficulties are our difficulties. We should like to know how we can help him. We seek his guidance in this matter"[34]. Thus, the hegemony of Nehru a political leader, was accepted. Probably,the constructive workers were unwilling to join issues with the political leaders. With his usual characteristic self-criticism, Vinoba blamed the constructive workers for their failure in carrying out constructive activities. He said, "Some criticism has been voiced here against the Government. It is, however, wrong to think that the Government is against constructive work. For example, it is our duty to make Khadi self-reliant. If we fail to do so, it will be our failure, not of the Government's".[35]

The agreement between the political and constructive workers on the basic principle of Sarvodaya was stressed. Nehru said, "I am one with Vinoba that our means should be as pure as the end. I am convinced beyond a shadow of doubt that wrong methods always lead to wrong results. If we are clear about this fundamental idea, all our questions can be resolved satisfactorily." All were agreed that the country's basic problem was "moral and spiritual".[36] There was also affirmation of mutual good will. Vinoba said, "I do not look on Pandit Jawaharlal Nahru as a representative of the Government, I regard him as a member of the Gandhian family".[37] To which Nehru replied, "please do regard me as one of your camp followers", and he held out the assurance: "I shall try my best to assist you in implementing the decisions of this conference".[38]

The Congress extended its support to constructive activities and to Bhoodan movement when it was launched. The AICC issued several circulars to all the provincial Congress committees asking them "to do their best for the success of the Bhoodan Yagna". All Pradesh Congress committees were instructed to constitute a special Bhoodan department and to take important Sarvodaya workers of the area on its executive board. The Avadi session of the Congress adopted a resolution on Bhoodan and Sampattidan i.e. gift of wealth in 1955:

The Congress, at its Hyderabad session, had warmly welcomed the Bhoodan movement started by Acharya Vinoba Bhave. During the last two years, the movement has been able to achieve substantial results by collecting about 36 lakh acres of land and steps are now being taken to redistribute it as expeditiously as possible.

The Bhoodan and Sampattidan movement, apart from tackling certain economic problems, is essentially a moral movement for bringing about a socio-economic revolution voluntarily and through peaceful means. The Congress places on record its deep sense of appreciation of the great work done by Acharya Vinoba and appeals to all Congressmen to give their fullest co-operation to this movement.[39]

Many state governments passed Bhoodan Yagna land legislation to legliaze the transfer of land, and co-operation between community development projects and Gramdan was worked out in various states; the government extended credit to Gramdan villages, the Planning Commission set aside Rs. 1 crore as a special fund in 1957 to be disbursed to the Gramdan areas as an interim measure so that, pending state legislation, Gramdan villages could go ahead with their development schemes. Moreover, several government welfare programmes, such as tribal development work, cottage industry, Khadi rehabilitation, basic education, relief work etc. have been carried out through Sarvodaya agencies, and their workers.

The Sarvodaya and Congress approaches to the land problem were not seen as conflicting but rather as complementary. The Gramdan conference in 1957 at Yelwal noted : "The members of the Central and state governments who were present, while expressing their full appreciation of the Gramdan movement and their desire to help it, pointed out that the Governments concerned would have to proceed with the schemes of land reforms which were for the abolition of all intermediate interests in land, the limitation of holding and the promotion of the co-operative movement in all its phase with the consent of the people concerned. This government approch was not in conflict with the Gramdan movement and would indeed be helped by it."[40]

The relation between the Congress and Sarvodaya was functionally positive. Shriman Narayan, a Gandhian leader, believes that "without the solid support of the Congress the Bhoodan movement would not have made much headway in the country".[41] Vinoba sent a message to the Avadi Congress session, "Tell them (delegates) on my behalf that a person is constantly moving about in the hope that all of them will run to his succour some day or other, and he deems himself entitled to receive their help".[42] A survey found that 72 per cent of the Sarvodaya workers considered the Congress to be the most sympathetic to Sarvodaya ideals.[43] Among those who exercised their voting right in elections in 1962, 81 per cent voted for the Congress.

During the 1950s relations between Nehru and Vinoba were cordial. Nehru attended some Sarvodaya conference, and Vinoba sent messages to some AICC sessions. Nehru used to consult Vinoba on several issues, particularly in respect of India's relations with the neighbouring countries. Sarvodaya workers were taken on several state and district planning and advisory committees of the Government. Although the Sarvodaya leaders did not approve of many policies such as the industrial policy, education and electoral system, they did not make an issue of them. The parting of ways first became visible in the sixties. In 1964, Nehru, anxious to seek Vinoba's advice in regard to several problems connected with Pakistan, China and Kashmir, repeatedly invited him to visit Delhi. For the first time Vinoba's response was negative. After Nehru's death in 1964, no Prime Minister has attended Sarvodaya Conferences, and no leading Sarvodaya worker has attended Congress sessions. Though Mrs. Gandhi had met Vinoba on several occasions, before 1975, the meetings had been more in the nature of courtesy calls than to have discussions on vital issues concerning the country. JP felt that Sarvodaya had come to be regarded by the Congressmen as "a crankish and fashion creed !"[44]

Actual confrontation of Sarvodaya workers with Congress governments began after the Congress split in 1969. In the beginning they were baffled between the moralist postu reof the Congress (O) and the radical posture of the Congress. The manipulative politics of Mrs. Gandhi added fuel to the fire. Sarvodaya workers who believe themselves to be the upholders of moral principles felt that "disregard for the purity of means in public life has led to all round degradation in moral standards."[45]

4. SPLIT IN SARVA SEVA SANGH

By the early seventies Vinoba was slowly retiring to background, and Jayaprakash Narayan was coming to the front of the Sarvodaya movement. Vinoba and JP, as mentioned earlier, differed in their approach to politics. And, JP was slowly taking more and more interest in politics—not as an onlooker and distant critic or the "India's conscience-keeper' in international sphere, but as an active non-party fighter against the ruling Congress. Under his influence, the Executive Committee of the Sarva Seva Sangh expressed its serious concern over national, economic and political issues, such as poverty, unemployment, violation of constitutional provisions, increasing concentration of power etc. Further, the Sarva Seva Sangh called a special convention at Sevagram on September 18 to 20, 1973 to review the national situation. It expressed its serious concern over 'the present situation' in the country. The problems of the country, according to the convention, were due to the departure of the Congress party from Gandhian principles and methods. It concluded that, "the present critical situation can be tackled only by strengthening peoples power...the awakening of political consciousness in the millions of the people, organizing them and offering resistance to injustice."[46] It gave a call to popular organizations to mobilize people and launch movements, especially for eradicating corruption and bribery. It called upon peasants, workers, youth, and women-folk "to give a new leadership to the country".

Further, some of the Sarvodaya workers supported the students' agitation of 1974 in Gujarat as a crusade against "corrupt politics". Ravishankar Maharaj, a prominent and respected Sarvodaya leader of Gujarat, made efforts to guide the agitation. Jayaprakash Narayan visited Gujarat and complimented the students.

In Bihar some young Sarvodaya workers had started a campaign and taken out processions to protest against price rise soon after the Sewagram conference. But they threw themselves into the movement when JP was persuaded to lead it. The second rank leadership of the movement was provided by Sarvodaya workers, and they held responsible positons at all levels. They chalked out the programmes; they mobilized the people; and they guided the students, always taking care that the movement did not get out of their hands. Several Sarvodaya workers from different parts of the country visited Bihar during the first year of the movement, quite a few of them spent three to eight months for organizing the struggle.

However, the participation of the Sarvodaya workers in the Bihar movement had brought about a split in the Sarva Seva Sangh. Vinoba and his supporters, who were in minority, were against 'politiclisation' of the Sangh. They insisted that the Sarvodaya movement stood for 'the spiritualisation of politics'. They also opposed the agitational approach followed by JP and his supporters.[47] They believed that the demand for the dissolution of the 'lawfully elected Assembly' was a political demand and against 'the value system ingrained in Sarvodaya ideology'. R.K. Patil, a supporter of the Vinoba line, said "His (JP's) movement is therefore essentially political in the sense that it seeks to capitalize on the people's grievances without providing any constructive avenues for their removal. In trying to build up agitation and dissatisfaction against the government, he is acting exactly as a leader of an opposition political party".[48] The struggle approach of JP, according to him, is a deviation from the constructive Gram Swarajya approach, and it "will shatter the Gandhian ideals beyond repair".

Jayaprakash Narayan, on the other hand, strongly advocated people's peaceful struggle to control the state power. He thought that the Gram Swarajya approach failed to solve the problems of land distribution. Defending his support to the demand for the dissolution of the State Assembly, JP explained, "Speaking for myself, I feel that I would have betrayed my responsibilities as a citizen if I had not fully supported the demand for the resignation of such a Ministry, and dissolution of such an Assembly. If the Sarvodaya philosophy stands in the way of my acting in this manner, I at least repudiate such an interpretation of that philosophy. In fact, my understanding of my responsibilities as a Sarvodaya worker is that I must raise my voice as strongly and act as effectively as possible to condemn and fight against such abuse of democratic power and democratic institutions".[49]

Though most of the members of the Sarva Seva Sangh supported JP's stand, there was no unanimity. And since according to the Sangh rules no decisions can be taken that are not unanimous, the activities of the Sangh were frozen for a year. Vinoba withdrew his membership from the organization which he himself had founded, and decided to observe silence for one year. A few of the pro-JP supporters started ridiculing Vinoba.

On the other hand, JP and his supporters begun reinterpreting some of the cardinal principles of Sarvodaya ideology. He made a distinction between 'non-violent' and 'peaceful' means : while non-violent means rules out secrecy, peaceful means does not. He characterised the Bihar movement as "peaceful" rather than "non-violent", JP allowed some of his followers to work underground. A few Sarvodaya workers warned JP that violence would erupt during the three days of October bandh. Inevitably violence did take place. JP held the CPI, Congress and Central Reserved Police (CRP) responsible for the violence. And, he declared that the bandh was "peaceful". Not all Sarvodaya workers agreed with the fine distinction that JP, made between peaceful and non-violent means. J.R. Sahni, a Sarvodaya worker, said, "in fact, only a non-violent struggle could also be peaceful and vice versa. There is not the slightest contradiction between the two".[50]

The sacred concept of the Sarvodaya philosophy, non-violence, also came up for re-examination. Haridwar Pandye, a Sarvodaya worker and an active worker in the movement, said, "In reality, violence and non-violence are not contradictory to each other. They are part of each other. They are two sides of the same coin. They are essential aspects of any society and nation. No idea or programme can only be violent or non-violent. Everywhere there is a mixture of violence and non-violence. The difference is only in degree: but less violence or more violence... violence can be decreased but cannot be completly removed".[51] It appears that Pandye was speaking for quite a few young Tarun Shanti Sena workers.

All the pro-JP Sarvodaya workers, however, were not happy with Jayaprakash's support to the "Janata Morcha" in the 1975 Gujarat Assembly elections. They became uneasy when JP appealed to the Gujarat voters to vote blindly for the Janata Morcha. They considered that it was not the front of the Janata. In Gujarat, most of the Sarvodayaists remained indifferent to the elections, though, in deference to their leader and much against their own inclination, they voted for the Morcha. This may well be an index of the lack of complete unanimity even among that section of Sarvodaya workers which had chosen to throw its support behind Jayaprakash Narayan. All this means that unanimity of views among the majority section of Sarvodaya movement was only an illusion.

CONCLUSION

The Sarvodaya ideology has many contradictions, and they come to the surface when Sarvodaya workers try to deal with empirical reality. Yet, they are all of one mind in their opposition to both capitalism and communism. The Bhoodan movement was born at the time of the communist upsurge in Andhra; and the Bihar struggle drew in JP when the communist forces were gathering strength in Bihar with their efforts to organize the poor for resisting exploitation. JP took up the leadership to eliminate forces which did not believe in *Sadhan Suddhi*, and whose ways of struggle were different from those of the Sarvodayaists.[52]

Although the Sarvodaya ideology stands for revolution, in actual practice it has so far helped the perpetration of *status quo*. The insistence on class collaboration and *Sadhan Suddhi* have so far helped the landed class, businessmen and other sections of the rich, and helped to nullify the struggle of the poor against the exploiters, though against the wishes of the Sarvodayaists. The impact of all the Bhoodan, Gramdan, Sulabh Gramdan movements etc. are negligible in terms of restructuring the society. The hearts of the rich have not changed, and for all the Sarvodaya stress on moral conduct, "immorality" now envelops the entire society, not wholly excluding Sarvodaya workers.

Thus, the Sarvodaya concept and the manner in which it has been put into practice by the majority section of the organization needs a through re-assessment and re-examination. But as the line between "missionary spirit" and "fanaticism" is very thin, they hope against hope that "some way out may still be found". They complacently cling to their pet theories and precepts and console themselves that the path to the search for truth is always strewn with thorns.

NOTES

1. Quoted by Shriman Narayan, *Vinoba : His Life and Work*, Bombay, Popular Prakashan, 1970.
2. Ibid.
3. *Everyman's*, January 26, 1975.

4. Ibid.
5. Ibid.
6. Ibid.
7. Quoted by Ajit Bhattacharjea, *Jayaprakash Narayan*, Delhi, Vikas Publishing House Pvt. Ltd., 1975.
8. Geoffrey Ostergaard, and Melville Currell, *The Gentle Anarchists*, London, Clarendon Press, 1971.
9. *Everyman's*, January 12, 1974.
10. Austin, *Cornerstone of Indian Constitution*, Bombay, Oxford University Press, 1972.
11. *Everyman's*, January 12, 1974.
12. Ibid., January 26, 1975.
13. Sriman Narayan,. op. cit.
14. Ibid.
15. Vinoba Bhave, *Revolutionary Sarvodaya*, Bombay, Bharatiya Vidya Bhavan, 1964.
16. Landed and Landless in Surat District. virtual class war, *Economic and Political Weekly*, June 22, 1974.
17. Sriman Narayan, op. cit.
18. Ibid.
19. Ibid.
20. Ibid.
21. Ibid.
22. K.R. Nanekar and S.V. Khandenvala, *Bhoodan and the Landless*, Bombay, Popular Prakashan, 1973.
23. Quoted by Mohan Ram, The Sarvodaya Farce, *Economic and Political Weekly*, May 3, 1975.
24. *The Indian Express*, July 13, 1974.
25. Geoffrey Ostergaad, Prelude To The Bihar Movement: Sarvodaya And the Search For Non Violent Revolution In India (mimiographed) Birmingham, Department of Politics. The University of Birmingham, 1976.
26. Ostergad and Currell, op. cit.
27. Geoffrey Ostergaad, op. cit.
28. The issue of their (Sarvodaya workers) dependance on government had been often discussed among the Sarvodaya workers. The Gram Swaraj workers' conference in 1972 accepted Nirmala Deshpande's position, who wanted no conflict with the government and pleaded for effective coordination between the movement's and government's programmes for rural development, even if this involved making compromises, see G. Ostergaad op. cit, also see Sriman Narayan op. cit.
29. I.P. Desai and B. Choudhry, *History of Rural Development in Modern India*, New Delhi, Impex India, 1977.
30. See, Minoo Masani, Jayaprakash Narayan, *Encounter*, December, 1975.

31. Laxminarayan Lal, *Jayaprakash* (Hindi), New Delhi, Macmillan, 1974.
32. Quoted Ibid.
33. Sriman Narayan, op. cit.
34. Ibid.
35. Ibid.
36. Ibid.
37. Ibid.
38. Ibid
39. Ibid
40. Ibid.
41. Ibid.
42. Ibid.
43. Ostergaad and Currell, op .cit
44. Ajit Bhattacharjea, op. cit.
45. *Convention on National Situation* Sevagram 18*th* to 20*th September*, 1973 *Statement*, Wardha, Secretary, Sarva Seva Sangh, 1973.
46. Ibid.
47. For detail see, Geoffrey Ostergaad, op. cit.
48. Symposium on Democracy in India: The trauma and the traveil *Gandhi Margh*, January 1975.
49. *Everyman's*, June 15, 1974.
50. A symposium on Democracy in India, op. cit.
51. *Sampuran Kranti ki Anivaryata, Uddeshya, Sidhant Aur Karyakram* (Hindi) Purana Bhojpur, Sampurna Kranti Navsahitya Rachana Evam Prakashan Samiti Karyalaya, 1974.
52. *Vatvruksha* (Gujarati, Vedchhi), June 1975.

5

Revolution, Reform or Protest

We have examined different aspects of the Bihar movement in the preceding chapters. We shall now discuss how far it is a revolutionary movement.

The Bihar movement aimed at bringing about Total Revolution, i.e. a revolution in social, economic, political, cultural and all other aspects of life. It declared that "the crux of the matter is that the movement is basically one against the *existing system*".[1] [emphasis added]. We do not expect Jayaprakash or his followers to spell out their concept of the Total Revolution and offer the scheme of an alternative social order for which they were striving. We can, therefore, only evaluate the movement from what it did ; we can judge it from its ideology, organization, leaders, cadre, and programmes on issues.

The ideoloy which guided the Bihar movement was the Sarvodaya ideology. The working of the Sarvodaya movement of the last twenty-five years has not produced or even set itself in the direction of any revolutionary changes in society. In fact, it has produced results exactly the opposite of those expected by the Sarvodayaists themselves. This is not because of the 'inability' of certain individuals or lack of 'commitment' on the part of the Sarvodaya workers. It is primarily because of the deficiencies of the ideology itself. We have seen that the contradictions of the Sarvodaya ideology came out sharply within the movement itself.

Moreover, most of the constituent partners of the Bihar movement did not share the ideology of the Sarvodayaists. They did not want revolution. Unlike Sarvodayaists, they were clear on this point. They were primarily interested in dethroning the Congress government and seizing political power for themselves.

The programmes of the movement did not concretize the objectives of the movement. Most of the programmes so far were mobilising programmes to create a tempo for the movement. The participants of these programmes did not get involved in other programmes. During the latter part of 1974 and thereafter, the mobilising programmes were undertaken mainly to show to Mrs. Gandhi and others outside Bihar that the movement had not fizzled out.

The movement had side-tracked economic issues and raised political and moral issues. The suggestions on electoral reforms looked to the convenience of the opposition parties rather than spelt out ways of curbing money power so as to revolutionize the electoral system. Similarly, JP's "revolutionary" education offered nothing more than the courses offered by the present-day universities and private coaching institutes. His crusade against corruption touched only the symptoms and not the disease. He ignored the corruption of his supporters and attacked only the Congress Party. The issues aroused only emotions.

Despite all denials, the dissolution of the Assembly had become an end in itself. There were no socio-economic programmes to be implemented after the dissolution. Like the party in power, the leaders of the movement seemed to be saying: Give us power and the rest will follow.

Depite contrary experiences and evidences, the Sarvodayaists believe that the state is neutral as between different sections of society. JP admitted that "we were wrong in this assumption and that the state system was subservient to a variety of forces with their interests entrenched in keeping it a closed shop is glaringly apparent now".[2] Yet, in the Bihar movement, we can see that the groups, classes or interests which dominated the Congress programmes were the same that support the movement. How could then one have expected the movement to bring about Total Revolution ?

Students were the vanguard of the Bihar movement. As a group they fited well in the class-collaboration theory of Sarvodaya. They are not earning, hence they are not in the economic market; they do not have a vested interest in society. They do not have any animosity against any class. Moreover, the Sarvodaya leaders accept the theory of 'generation gap' and believe that students do not approve of the values, customs and institutions of their parents. Therefore, they can become the agents of change in society. Sensitive and vocal and having no family responsibilities, students can afford to be full-time revolutionaries.

That students do not have the class character of their family is wishful thinking. The issues that the students of Bihar and Gujarat took up during the agitations were concerned with the class to which they belonged. Clashes among students in the campuses are often based on class or caste conflicts. It is true that students revolt against their parents, but not because of a clash of values and norms. Empirical studies point out that students do not differ in values with their parents except in matters of dress and sex relations. Ironically enough, Sarvodayaists do not agree with students' norms regarding drees and sex. Students accept the caste system, the caste customs, the economic structure etc. This is the reason why JP's call for changes in social customs received a cold response. The student leaders, who largely come from the upper and middle classes, are careerists; they are concerned with jobs, better prospects and material comforts in life. Therefore, they joined colleges in large numbers against JP's advice. Moreover, students are not familier with the intricacies of social problems. They hardly feel that the socio-economics and political systems are unjust. It is true that the students are vocal and sensitive; they have revolted against political authority in Gujarat, Thailand, France and elsewhere. But revolt is not revolution. Students are after all a floating population, one ceases to be a student in four or five years in the universities. And revolution cannot come in four years.[3]

The Sarvodaya workers and their supporters banked upon Janata, i.e. the people, to bring about a revolution. They formed Jana Sangharsh Samiti, Janata Sarkar, and Janata Morcha. But who was this Janata ? They ignored this question because it was against the Gandhian philosophy. To them, Janata includes all and everybody. But in reality, their Janata was only confined to urban upper and middle class, landlords and neo-rich farmers who form a small section of the total population. These were the people who supported and parti-

cipated in the movement. They are the people who are benefited in different degrees by the present system. They want
more benefits by bringing about certain changes in the system.
They do not believe in changing the basic aspects of the system.
They have a stake in the system. To them Revolution is a
slogan. Whenever JP had taken the slightest radical
stand in favour of workers and have-nots, the same Janata
which carried JP on their shoulders, backed out and did not
hesitate to call him a confused person out to create class conflicts in society. This Janata was not for any kind of revolution.
And the other Janata stood bewildered; it was outside the
movement.

It is argued that "the beginning and end of every revolution
is characteristically political, in the sense that it begins with
a political crisis and ends with political settlement".[4] This is
true. But the important question is : what kind of political
settlement ? And in whose favour ? It appears that the political settlement that the Bihar movement leading to was the
settlement for *status quo* in favour of the haves. Looking
through the programmes, the leadership, and the cadre, it
appears that the Bihar movement did not have the potentialities of a revolutionary movement.

Jayaprakash Narayan himself said. "This movement is
within the party system, within the Constitution, within the
framework of the People's Representation Act. I will be very
happy if reform takes place but I do not expect miracles to
happen"[3]. The movement thus, at the most, strived for some
reforms in the electoral system, in the system of education, in
economic planning and in social customs.

Even as a reform movement, the Bihar agitation suffered
from major limitations. First, it had the illusion that it was a
revolutionary movement. The leaders of the movement therefore did not concentrate on reformist demands. Second, the
movement desired to bring reforms in all aspects of life.
Hence, there was confusion and failure to concentrate on a few
aspects with a clarity of purpose. Third, the movement had
become a political struggle. Fourth, the cadre of the movement were not trained to run and expand a reform movement.

The Bihar movement was a protest movement, protesting
against the failure of the Congress rule in delivering the goods.

It ventilated dissatisfaction and grievances of large sections of society. The partners of the movement used the upsurge of the people for dethroning the Congress. The Sarvodaya workers who had Revolution at their heart was not interested in seizing political power to reshape the socio-political and economic order. And the political parties were not interested in Revolution. To them, Total Revolution was another catchy slogan like that of Garibi Hatao was to win elections. After the elections, they would say good-bye to the movement, (as the Congress did to Mahatma in 1947) leaving JP and Sarvodaya workers high and dry for introspection and expiation.

NOTES

1. *Everyman's*, November 9, 1974.
2. Ibid,, April 27, 1975.
3. However, we need to make distinction between the students as a class or group and individual students. As a class, the students do not have potentialities to bring about revolution. But at the same time, sensitive students can be drawn in the movement to build cadres and organization and to mobilise other sections of society.
4. J.D. Sethi, Jayaprakash Narayan and his revolution, *Gandhi Marg,* January 1975.
5. *The Hindustan Times*, August 26, 1974.

POSTSCRIPT

The foregoing study is conflicted to one year of the Bihar movement. The study was completed in June 1975, on the eve of the internal Emergency. Since then various political changes have taken place in the country. Nevertheless, I do not feel any need to change or modify the earlier analysis. I have kept as it was written in June 1975. It should be underscored that the focus of the study is on the 'total revolution' aspect of the movement.

However, since the post-June 1975 events are extra-ordinary in the political history of the country, I give a brief resume of the events in the context of the Bihar movement.

As the nation's economy was deteriorating fast and sporadic upsurge of the poor masses threatened law and order situation the ruling party found it difficult to manage the country. The Allahabad High Court verdict against Mrs. Indira Gandhi's election and the direct action launched by various opposition parties and Sarvodaya workers under the leadership of Jayaprakash Narayan threatened the congress rule. That accelerated the process of authoritarianism and repression of the activities of the opposition parties.

Besides several others, a large number of the rank and file of the Bihar movement and its leaders, including Jayaprakash Narayan were detained under MISA or DIR. A few of them went underground. A state of fear prevailed, and in the absence of the leadership the movement came to a halt.

On January 18, Mrs. Gandhi dissolved the fifth Lok Sabha and annouced new election. Most but not all political detenus were released. Congress (O), Jana Sangh, Bhartiya Lok Dal and Socialists formed the Janata Party under the guidance of JP. They reached an electoral alliance with other parties also to give a straight fight to the Congress. Under the leadership of Jagjivan Ram, a section of the Congress leaders left the party. They formed the Congress For Democracy (CFD). This gave a big jolt to the Congress and strengthened the anti-Congress forces. That also helped the mobilization of the Scheduled Castes in many places against the Congress.

The Janata Party issued its manifesto containing a good deal of Sarvodaya ideology. JP and Sarvodaya workers worked actively in campaigning for the Janata Party. For the first time since Independence, they participated actively in electoral politics. They were determinant to defeat the Congress. Like other parties, the main consideration in the selection of Janata Party condidates was their capacity to win the election, hence party, caste, community, region, capacity to spend money were given weightage over individual's political conviction and past record. Also the process of selection was centralised rather than decentralised. In Bihar the Chhatra Sangharsh Samiti (BCSS) demanded tickets for students, but only one got it. They were promised that they would be given tickets in the state Assembly elections. The Congress is completely routed in Bihar and other Hindi-speaking areas.

The election results are interpreted by many politicians, Sarvodaya workers and academicians as the victory of democracy over dictatorship. This is an oversimplified interpretation. This interpretation leads us to an erroneous inference, that some states are for democracy and other states are for Emergency, if not for dictatorship. Election results have to be analysed in the context of each state.

Be that as it may, Jayaprakash Narayan has emerged as the leader of the new wave. The Janata and CFD members of Parliament took an oath under his leadership at Rajghat to observe austerity and build the nation on the Gandhian model. Jayaprakash took the "concensus" of the party, and declared Morarji Desai, a Gandhian as India's new Prime Minister. The Sarvodaya workers have once again come closer to the government as they were during the fifties under Nehru's primership. Questions arise : Would they once again break away from politics for constructive work? Would the Sarvodayaists become politicians like other politicians? It seems that they have no obtion but to participate in politics.

INDEX